AFRICAN PROVERBS AND MEANINGS

A Compilation Of The
Greatest African Proverbs
And Their Meanings.

Sylvanus. NJ

A collection of proverbs from;

Nigeria

Egypt

Ghana

South Africa

Algeria

Congo

Tanzania

Kenya

Rwanda

Senegal

Zimbabwe

Zambia

Uganda

Burundi

Niger

Ivory Coast

Morocco

Sierra Leone and more African countries....

Introduction

This book is a collection of wise sayings from across Africa, each with a clear meaning.

African proverbs are more than just words; they are rich with life lessons and cultural values. They are shared in moments of joy and sorrow, offering guidance and reflection.

In this book, you'll find proverbs from different African cultures, each with its meaning explained. These sayings provide timeless wisdom and a glimpse into African life and traditions.

Enjoy exploring these proverbs and the lessons they offer. Let them inspire and guide you, connecting you to the heart of African wisdom. Ubuntu!

Guide to the book

This book of African proverbs and meanings was thoughtfully written to educate, enlighten and offer Africa to the world through its rich and great proverbs.

The writer, Sylvanus NJ is a Nigerian poet and student of history who teamed up with Kandi Mapuwa from Congo, Malick from Egypt, Lutoyo from Kenya, Samuel from Ghana and Mapundiwa from Rwanda to compile and interpret these great proverbs.

The proverbs in the book was purposely scattered among countries to give readers a sense of adventure, suspense and fascination to read.

Some proverbs may slightly not appear to politically incorrect. However, you have to focus on the wisdom in the pages of this book and respect the diverse cultures of this vast continent.

If you educate a man, you have educated an individual but if you educate a woman, you have educated a community.

This ancient Congolese proverb teaches the importance of women in African societies at large. Right before the inception of gender equality and feminism, some African regions had understand the importance of an educated woman who will in turn pass her education to the children because she is the one who spends more time with them, hence, it is expected that the children will learn directly from them while they grow. From the analogy of this proverb; the education might not necessarily be formal education, it could be knowledge of medicinal herbs and roots, fashion and arts, entertainment, house welfare and more.

So, as the world is grappled with the gender equality and feminism saga, we must understand that men and women are like the two hands, it works well when both are working and supporting each other. So, we must be careful and campaign for the positives and be careful not to radicalize the awareness and turn it to the right hand versus the left hand instead of the left hand working with the right hand for the common good of all.

Congolese proverb

The day the blind man sees, the first thing he will throw away is that same walking stick that has been his eyes.

We must know that our usefulness to people will be outlived one day. We must know that the world doesn't revolve around us, yes, it doesn't, and you are not that important to the natural occurrences of things.

Every parent must know that once their child gets married, their importance decreases in terms of stipulating how the child lives. Same thing is applicable to a mentor or teacher. Believe me, there will come a time your role will be to sit back and watch your students' progress because if we fail to understand this; time will come when they will see you as the burden.

Also, this ancient Ethiopian proverb teaches us to understand that there will come a time we will need to gradually start letting go of those we have been catering for so they will learn to carry their own jar of water and not totally become dependent us.

Ethiopian proverb

To get the gold, you must first dig and soil yourself.

Nothing in life comes easy. You don't build castles in the thin air and expect to live in in it. There is a price to pay for greatness in life. Sacrifices has to be made, efforts has to be made, consistency has to be maintained, passion and dedication must be in play, and one must not consider giving up until the desired success is attained. You must dig in, soil your clothes, take breaks if necessary but you must keep digging to get to your gold because the great things of life always hide behind hard work. The price you must pay to get them is hard work.

This concept is also applied in all ramifications of life, to be a great athlete; you must consistently out-train others and live a healthy life. To be a great surgeon, you must out-study others to be the greatest. To be a great lawyer, you must out-study and outsmart others. To be a good programmer, you must practice more than others. To be a great artist, you must practice more than others and learn from the greats. You must give in something to obtain something in life; such is the rule of life. Nothing is free.

Egyptian proverb

He who stops building his house because a nail broke was never ready to build one.

He who doesn't go to farm because the weather gets moody anytime he wants to go to the farm will have nothing to harvest doing harvest time and his family will starve. Excuses and excuses and more excuses are simply the language of the lazy and useless man.

The proverb is used to admonish people to look beyond whatever they feel hinders them from their aspirations and work under sweat and cold to achieve their dreams before they become old and frail and die as a failed person.

Gambian proverb

It is the mouth that gives thanks for today that will be fed tomorrow.

Gratitude paves way for more favors and giving.

This very powerful Tanzanian proverb teaches the very important act of being gracious for the little and big things that we have. The proverb is used by elders to teach the younger ones that they should be appreciative people in their daily endeavors. They use it to teach the youths that gratitude to someone that shows them generosity or rendered them any kind of help simply motivates this helper to do more. So, it is very wise that we find ways to make people understand that you see their efforts, gifts, grace, helps and that you truly appreciate them.

Tanzanian proverb

The farmer whose seeds have not germinated does not give up planting.

Persistency, consistency and dedication will help you achieve your dreams.

With the analogy which is self-explanatory we understand the power of consistency and hard work.

The world doesn't work like the movies, you don't get lucky and win a lottery and become a millionaire overnight. The world works in an effort and outcome concept, you have to put in the work required to get that which you want. You have to be consistent until you see the results, you mustn't give up on your dreams for it is achievable, you simply have to believe and work for it.

Kenyan proverb

The great king's child is also a slave in another king's land.

The world doesn't revolve around anyone. You are not that important. With or without you, the wheels of life will continue rolling. So, stay humble, treat others as you would love to be treated because you could be a king in your place but a commoner in another place.

So, as the proverb implies, we all must live our lives with the outmost humility, empathy and compassion for the less privileged while keeping a good name because it could pave way for us or our descendants later in life.

Rwandan proverb

One must prepare now for the solutions of tomorrow's troubles.

Just like other African proverbs; they all in one way or the other tries to prepare the young for tomorrow. This one isn't far from the point either as it teaches that we must as a matter of fact prepare for our tomorrow today. It teaches that we mustn't relent to prepare ourselves for the later days of our lives while we are still youth and strong. It teaches us that we have our youthful stages in life to determine how we will live out our days as old and retired people.

Tanzanian proverb

The smelly words of the elderly will become sweet someday if listened to.

This Sudanese proverb teaches the young that it is always wise to listen to the advice of those that have had experiences in the things they want to do in life. It also teaches that although they might sound old fashioned or stressful, they sure know what they are saying of which when listened to and followed, you will not make the same mistakes they made. So, in other words, mentors are important in life as they will help the young get to their desired destination in career, education, entertainment, athletics and other aspects of life faster and with fewer hurdles on the way.

It is paramount that youths seek out mentors, especially in their fields so they can learn off of someone who has been there, seen it and done it.

Sudanese proverb

The hippopotamus never dances with the monkeys.

One must know their place in life. One must know their role and play accordingly.

This wise Zulu proverb teaches the importance of not missing with the wrong crowd or following the wrong mix of people.

As a student of law, it is unwise that your mixtures of friends are engineering students. As an athlete, your larger mixture of friends cannot be rappers and thugs. You must as a matter of fact follow the right circle that shares similar philosophy, struggle, ambition and drive with you. Know your place today and make the necessary adjustments if necessary.

South African proverb

If you are ugly, you must learn to dance or be a good love maker.

You cannot be useless in everything in life. You must know how to understand your weaknesses and maximize them and turn them to strengths.

The proverb teaches us that excuses and laziness will not put food on our table or give us a name. One must look beyond their limitations and aim for success. Your destiny is in your hands, no heavenly angel is coming to give you lottery ticket in your dream because you fast and go to church every day. You must find a way to survive to and succeed in life.

Tanzanian proverb

No beautiful tattoo is accomplished without the sight of blood and pain.

Life is never a bed of rose and pearls. No good thing comes from wishful desires, a price has to be paid and paid in full.

To get a diamond, one must toil, soil his clothe, sweat and consistently dig while believing that he will see diamond to be able to eventually get one. Sometimes, he might dig for days, weeks, months without seeing but he will eventually find one and the hard work will be worth it.

Pay the price to achieve your dreams today. Work hard for it and you will attain it with time.

Zimbabwean proverb

A frail canoe doesn't know who the king is when it turns over. Everyone in it gets wet.

This Zambian proverb is used to warn the young ones about the dangers of societal decadence due to negligence and lack of communal relationship. The proverb teaches that when we neglect our duties to elect good leaders, look out for one another and participate in nation building; we will also be among those that will experience what bad leadership and policies looks like. As a matter of fact, this proverb encourages us all to join in any way possible to make our environment, families, communities, cities, groups, states and nations a better place to live and raise families because we will enjoy the benefits of a well-run place. However, if we neglect to play our own parts, economic crises, crimes and low quality of life will not exempt us from its claws.

Zambian proverb

Put out the fire when it is still small.

Timing is everything in life. This proverb teaches us the importance of understanding timing in everything we do in life. The proverb also teaches us that procrastination is never a good tool for one aiming to achieve greatness in life. We must as a matter of fact utilize each opportunity as it presents itself to us.

So, do that project today, read that book today, make that call today, send the text today. Do not procrastinate because it could be too late tomorrow. Just do it now.

Kenyan proverb

The water that was gotten from begging never quenches one's thirst.

This Ugandan proverb is so important that I feel it is one that we all must pay absolute attention to. The proverb is used to teach the young ones about the importance of doing their best while they are still young to make a life for themselves and succeed and have their own livelihood before old age comes and they start begging and looking up to others for aid. This proverb is telling us that although some will be generous to help but the help will never be enough because a loaf of bread can only serve the starving tummy for a day. Hence, it is vital that you position yourself to be able to afford the bread than beg for it. So, by all means morally and ethically good, find a way to survive and have your own reliable source of livelihood.

Ugandan proverb

One who has children never dies even after his burial.

This wise proverb is used to remind youths about the importance of procreation and family. Also, it is also used to teach people that one with a good name, reputation, integrity and compassion mostly lives in the heart of people even after death. According to the interpretation of the proverb, the children are those important virtues like integrity, generosity, compassion, trustworthy, reliability and reputation.

In a world where the strong and sacrosanct marriage institution of family of a father and mum with kids is being threatened by radicals, radical ideology mafias in many names and forms; we as a people must never allow these radicals win and we must continue to push for the protection of the marriage institution and procreation.

Algerian proverb

The roaring lion kills no prey but goes home empty.

This great African proverb is used to teach people about the importance of humility, strategy in life, not being boastful, not being loud or a talkative. Just imagine it; a lion that goes about in the jungle roaring, do you think it will be able to kill any prey? No, they will hear its roar and leave before it even comes close. Such is life too; we must refrain from being open book to people because of our talkativeness. It is ideal to achieve in silence and let your success make the noise. You never know who will wish you bad for your success, so keep them off their scheme by moving silently in your own lane.

South African proverb

No rain without waves.

Don't see a successful man and assume that he was just a lucky fellow. No, that is not the case, rather, he is successful because he understood what he wanted, put in the required hard work and consistency and achieved his aim.

Life and the attainment of greatness in it is never a thing of coincidence. Can you imagine the kind of bullying Elon Musk must have gotten from his peers while he isolated himself to work for the things he believed? However, he remained focused and determined to go after his dreams.

Hence, this proverb is used to admonish people to look beyond envy and work towards self-actualization because there is no Angel going around handing out greatness to those that don't want to put in the required hard work and consistency.

Malawian proverb

He who cannot dance will say that the drum is bad.

This great proverb teaches us to be weary of whom we employ to do services for us. It also teaches us to look at ourselves in the mirror once we start making excuses for everything that we fail to accomplish. The lesson is that one often resorts to blame games and excuses when they cannot do a work. So, we should be ready to let go of such deadbeats or change methods if it happens to be us.

South African proverb

No mighty tree stands without its roots.

We all need proper beginnings. We all need a shoulder
to lean on when it gets tough. This shoulder can be
siblings, parents, friends, partners, mentors or our
children.

Also, this proverb teaches us that we need to start early
and properly to build our careers or whatever we want
to do in life lest we become hasty and build what will
not stand the test of time.

Congolese proverb

If a leader has a liking for you, he will make sure you build your house on the rock close to clean waters.

In as much as we shouldn't be sycophants and praise singers, we should also find ways to be in good relationships with people at places of authority.

This proverb is used to admonish the young ones that are still building their careers, still studying or whatever they are doing that is for their own greatness to befriend those that are in the position to make their jobs, studies, and activities in their fields easier.

You can't be at loggerheads with people that can make your life miserable. Humble yourself, stay focused and dedicated on what you want. Don't let pride and ego delay your rise in life.

Senegalese proverb

Both the old and new millet still ends up in the same mill.

This life is simply a market, everyone comes and buys what they want and goes home. Life shouldn't be filled with hatred, envy, jealousy and wars. We should understand that we share more similarities than differences regardless of the continent we come from. No race or people are superior to others. Black, brown, yellow, white, pink, and whatever color that remains are all human. We shouldn't be hell-bent on dividing ourselves, rather uniting for the common good of everyone because kings, royalties and commoners came to earth the same way and we will all return to mother earth by death. No one will live forever.

So, show more compassion, be empathetic, and be more generous and kind for we all are one.

Niger proverb

We gradually become what we think about every day.

Our mind is our greatest asset in life.

The early Igbo ancestors understood the effects the mind has on the rest of the body, hence, they used this proverb to teach both the young and the old that they should be very careful of what they feed their mind in life because it will manifest in our life.

So, feed your mind positivity, faith in yourself, things that will help you grow in life, feed it with good books, good affirmations and let your thoughts be positive too and you will gradually see every other thing change for your good.

Nigerian proverb

**The fearsome bull will be overpowered
once it starts limping.**

This proverb teaches us to be careful of whom we
reveal our vulnerabilities to. We need to understand
that every smiling face doesn't necessarily want the
best for us. Some friends, siblings, colleagues and
mates are so devilish that they can go the extra mile
just to see us fall. Life is a very scary place, so we must
by all means know who we show our weaknesses to in
life lest they use it against us.

Ethiopian proverb

He who learns from others must also teach others.

Those who have learnt how to make life better in any capacity must endeavor to pass the knowledge to others. Just like the Igbo apprentice system where young boys and girls comes to an already made trader to learn how to trade directly from the experienced trader and also serve them while learning the tricks of the market which they will never learn from formal education. And to cap it off, they are given financial backings and goods to start their own business once they have served for a certain number of years.

Another instance of this is mentorship system where experienced heads takes the newbies under their wings and teaches them some of the things that will help make their journey easy in life, especially in their career or while studying.

So, the bottom line here is that it is in the collective interest of us all that we try to impact any sort of valuable knowledge we have to the ones that look up to us.

Ethiopian proverb

So many small things makes a man love a woman in so many big ways.

This great Ghanaian proverb is mostly used by aged people to teach their daughters about the importance of good character, education, attitude, and homeliness.

We must make our ladies understand that no one wants to marry or keep a beautiful nonsense at home. What quality men wants from a woman they want to marry goes beyond fine face, big butts and curvy body. So, work on your intangibles today and let the appearances be secondary or complimentary to your real value.

Ghanaian proverb

Every door has its own key.

There is a price to pay for any greatness in life. To be an athlete, you must train your whole life, you must sacrifice your lifestyle to fit what you are doing, and you must stick to a diet others might not like.

To be a good medical doctor, the key to it is to sacrifice your time and dedicate it on studies after studies, practical after practical, research after research.

To be a computer programmer, the key to it is consistent programming, consistent time on your screen coding, learning, doing essential boot camps, and learning more.

To be a good engineer, the key to it is proper studies, practical, research, internship and mentorship.

There are keys for everything we dream about, we just need to know them so we can put an effort to get those keys and achieve them.

Kenyan proverb

**The shepherd that his sheep runs away
twice must be a fool.**

One must not allow adversity to befall them two times
because of their ignorance or negligence in life.

Learn to discern things and people that are not good
for your growth either financially, emotionally,
spiritually, academically or your life in general.

You need to be intentional in selecting friends,
partners and other things you want in life.

Egyptian proverb

You must not fear the forest because it is dense.

Your life is in it. Your food, herbs and protection lies in it. Do not be afraid to go after the things you want in life because the process of getting it seems challenging and difficult. Nothing great comes easily. You need to dig in deep because achieving those things determines if you will have food on your table tomorrow, if you will provide a better life for your family, if you will retire early and well. Your happiness depends on your level of success which is not necessarily money though. So strive to achieve those things that you desire and do not die of regrets because of things you could have done that you didn't do.

Congolese proverb

One head alone, no matter how wise doesn't go into council alone.

Your 6 might be another person's 9 in life. That is why it is often wise to look at situations from different angles. Do not be myopic in the way you deal with things in life. It is vital that you do the necessary consultations to know everything possible about anything you are doing first before embarking on it.

Ghanaian proverb

There is no rain season without mosquitoes.

Wealth comes with its headaches and challenges, poverty comes with its challenges, and each stage we attain in life comes with its headaches and challenges no matter how we try to avoid them. That is just life, hence, this proverb is teaching us to expect these problems and find a way to conquer them.

Congolese proverb

The rain recognizes no king; everyone gets equally drenched.

Life is a respecter of none. She has no regards for your feelings, sensitivity, challenges, disabilities, religion, race, political affiliations and preferences. She just deals with you as she wishes.

The knowledge in this Nigerian proverb is enormous because it teaches us to take life as we see it and do the best we can for ourselves and loved ones.

Everyone must experience some kind of heartbreak at least once in life. Everyone must experience the pain of loss of a loved one. Everyone must put in the work required to succeed. And at least, everyone must die. There is no escaping these things regardless of who you are.

Nigerian proverb

Those that achieve great things first paid attention to little ones.

It is often the little things that matters in character building and creation of wealth. It is those little habits and thoughts we have that shape our future most times.

This proverb teaches us to pay good attention to those things we spend most of our time thinking and doing because they will in one way or the other manifest in our life.

Malian proverb

The ultimate secret for a good health is a good head.

You are simply what you think.

This wise proverb teaches us that we must as a matter of fact endeavor to have a healthy and clear mind if we want to have a healthy and productive life.

One who has being through traumatic experiences will not have the fortitude to do anything because he is busy fighting the demons that live rent free in his head.

Yes, life can be so tough; especially loss of loved ones, partners, children, friends, pets, businesses or other bad experiences but you must make a decision. You must decide if you want to be consumed by your demons or if you want to conquer them and move on. Make that ultimate decision today. Don't enter into marriage if you have not healed from your trauma of being raised in a toxic home. Don't enter into any business if you are afraid because of your last venture failure. Don't enter any relationship if you have not healed from your past toxic relationship. Try, do what you can do and find a way to heal because your success and peace of mind greatly depends on it.

Somalian proverb

He who wants to fight a lion with a stick must have been tired of living

Yes, it is good to take risks in life but we must understand when we are becoming delusional so we may avoid taking uncalculated risks and meet or doom.

We must be realistic in whatever we are doing lest we go building palaces on the sky.

South African proverb

You must not tell the person carrying you that he stinks.

This proverb teaches the importance of gratitude and appreciation to those who are benevolent enough to render any sort of help to us in life.

We must not be ingrates because such lifestyle will only chase people away from us and leave us to suffer in life.

Be grateful, be cheerful, and be thankful for any help you get from anyone no matter how insignificant they may seem.

Sierra Leone proverb

A house that has no shame lacks honor.

This proverb speaks about integrity and good reputation and its importance in the life of everyone.

The house in the proverb is just an analogy because it stands for person.

In a world where wealth is the sole aim of existence of many. A world where ethics, morality and originality has become an expensive luxury, you can only imagine how that person that has a good name and reputation will be sought after in his field or career. No one has the energy to be investigating people's words, actions or intentions at work or in business. So imagine the joy they will derive from dealing with that fellow whose words are the simple truth and has no deceits or hidden agenda in it.

If you are the dishonest type, change your ways today and see how your life turns around for good.

Ethiopian proverb

Pretend you are dead and you will see those that truly love you.

This life is a crazy place. Everyone is after what they will get from you, dishonesty, fraud, criminality, lack of good ethics and morality is the norms now. A larger number of the people you deal with in a day are looking to exploit you for their selfish interests. So, it is only wise that you adhere to this great proverb which teaches us not to be so open like a book while dealing with people. According to it, we must use our initiative and think through whenever we are dealing with people.

No one must know everything about you, not even your partner. You must only reveal what is necessary and take others to your grave.

Also, the proverb teaches us to sometimes say no to those who always ask something of us and see if they are really interested in you as a person or for only what you can give.

Egyptian proverb

A single bracelet on the leg of the dancer never jingle.

This ancient Congolese proverb teaches us that we must as a matter of fact find a circle or even one like-minded individual who possess the same fire you have in any field of work you are in. There is strength in unity and cohesion. This world was not made for us to survive it alone. Yes, it is important to isolate sometimes but it is smarter to work as a unit, especially when everyone wants the same outcome.

Congolese proverb

A big fish can only be caught with big bait.

To achieve greatness in life, one must equally be willing to put in great hard work to make it happen.

This sweet Ghana proverb is used to teach people that nothing big in life comes easily. If you desire a certain level of success, you must equally put in the level of hard work, consistency and dedication required to make it happen. If you desire to be an international athlete, then you must outwork your local colleagues first, then you put in the level of dedication needed for the international colleagues and also try to outwork them too, so you can conquer them as well. In other words, you must be willing to put in the big level hard work. There is no two ways about it luck will not work, and prayers will not work here to. You simply have to put in the work.

Ghanaian proverb

Where you will stand in your old age shows where you stood as a youth.

This great proverb is used to teach people about the importance of hard work, starting early in life to build success, self-reliance and dependence and the need for everyone to maximize their youthfulness and make a life for their selves before they become old and unable to do much again.

The proverb seeks to inform the young ones that how they live their lives now that they are young and productive will determine the quality of life they will have when they become old and frail.

Nigerian proverb

A little rain a day will gradually make a river.

There is due process for every great thing in life.

One doesn't just wake up and become great in life. No, that is not how life works; instead there is a price of hard work, consistency, determination, dedication, self-improvement, humility, charisma, integrity and good name that must be paid to make it happen. And most importantly, patience has to be implored as well because it is a procedure. And believe me, it may take time but greatness waits.

Madagascar proverb

A child never laughs at the disability of his mother.

It is the name you call your dog that people will call it.

This proverb teaches the importance of respect, dignity and love for your siblings, parents, partners, business, and career, sources of income, and friends or children.

Learn to treat people in your life with the outmost respect and care you can so that outsiders will learn from you and accord them the same respect.

Guinea Bissau proverb

Rubies should be sold to those who know the true value.

Endeavor to align your interests with people that share similar values with you. Do business with individuals that are focused and interested in seeing your growth and the general growth of the venture.

The proverb teaches us to know our value as a person and enforce our boundaries so we will not attract classless people in our life that will come and play with our sanity.

Do not go low in life when selecting people around you. You need to be very intentional about your standards. However, you need to be realistic and not delusional about it.

Ivory Coast proverb

Being happy and having a peace of mind in your household with a happy wife and children is better than being a king with many riches and no friend.

This great Malian proverb teaches about the importance of good family institution and its benefits to the members and the society at large.

Nothing is more gratifying to a person than the idea and reality that he has a home, people that loves him without conditions and him to loves these people and will literally go to the ends of the world to provide and protect them.

I understand that some are not lucky enough to have experienced being raised in a loving home with loving parents and siblings, nonetheless, the truth remains that most enjoyed this great feeling of unconditional love from childhood to adulthood. So, it is a fact that none will love you more than your family. So, we should keep our egos aside and reconcile with them and let the powerful love of a family overwhelm you.

Malian proverb

The chameleon looks at both directions before it crosses the road. It's not flexing its neck, it has a reason.

Life is full of trails, challenges and many hurdles that are hell-bent on devouring you and making you a mediocre person. You must not rust easily in life. You must not assume that everyone wants the best for you because they smile in your face. Life is bigger and more complicated that. You need to understand that the man is trickery and evil most times.

The lesson in the proverb is that we should all be very cautious on how we deal with people and any other thing in life. We need to properly think about things before we commit.

South African proverb

Little by little, the bird builds its nest.

Greatness in life is not achieved by hasty decisions.
Most great things come to life with patience,
dedication and consistency. So, we need, as a matter of
fact be patience on our pursuit for greatness in life.

Take the necessary time required to attain the results
you want, you only need to be committed, dedicated,
and consistent in achieving the goal.

South African Proverb

He who refuses to obey can never command.

Respect is earned in life. You can never force people into respecting you through arrogance, unkindness, wickedness and pride.

To be a leader, you need to charm people into buying into your vision with your kindness, exemplary lifestyle, professionalism, charisma, integrity and services.

Congolese proverb

The chameleon changes color to match the earth but the earth never changes to match the chameleon.

Life has no regards for you and your feelings, your disability, limitations, your background, race, religion, and political affiliations. She is not interested in your troubles and shenanigans. She expects you to fight out your redemption, she expects you to find yourself and find your own way to survive.

So, this proverb teaches that life never cares about the things we face in it, instead, you must find your way to success and happiness.

Rwandan proverb

If an arrow doesn't penetrate the victim so deep, then its removal will not be hard.

Do not allow procrastination end you before you get up on your feet to do what is necessary. Never allow poverty, heartbreak or grief to get the best of you in life.

Yes, life can be challenging sometimes, sometimes it might seem that we are not trying even when we are outworking every other person in the room. However, we need to keep on pushing regardless of the challenges and delays we may face while going for our dreams.

Keep your heads up today and keep on fighting Soldier; I promise you it will all make sense one day.

Kenyan proverb

The child that doesn't clean his mouth before breakfast always tells his mother that she served him a sour food.

Sometimes we need to look at ourselves to find out if we are blaming the wrong people for our problems instead of ourselves. We often forget that we are the ones that make the decision that makes or breaks us in life.

So, this proverb is telling us to always look at the mirror first to see what the man in the mirror is saying before we start looking outside for the reasons behind our misfortunes.

Tanzanian proverb

One cannot climb to the top of Mount Kilimanjaro without crushing some weeds with his feet.

There comes a time in the life of a person when he puts himself first. Your happiness and peace of mind with the inclusion of security and welfare for yourself and loved ones are vital than gossips and assumptions of the insignificant people in your life.

There also comes a time in the life of a person when he needs to understand that it is alright to leave behind some certain people in life. It is alright to outgrow peers. It is alright to overgrow colleagues and more. You cannot make it to the top of the mountain or rather greatness in life without having haters, people who don't like you or who failed to manipulate you and then switch to gossips, envy and more.

Just focus on making yourself better with compassion, integrity, kindness and forget about what insignificant people are talking about.

Congolese proverb

Those who are born on the top of the anthill take a lot of time to grow tall.

This proverb is used to teach those that are fortunate enough to be born with a silver spoon to be very careful of how they see life lest they become lazy, complacent, and rude and doom their best friend.

The proverb understands how it is easy for people to become complacent when they have everything, even more than they needed anytime they desired it. Such people, especially for teenagers often assume that Daddy or Mummy's money and influence will shadow them even till old age.

Kenyan proverb

Even the most decorated and loved village dancer will one day retire.

There is time for everything in life and anytime lost is mostly not reclaimed again as time and tide waits for no one.

This proverb teaches the importance of the understanding of time and proper utilization of it.

The proverb also teaches people about the importance of planning for the rainy days in life. People should learn from the squirrels and gather nuts in their storage for preparation of the rainy days. So, as you work, learn to be prudent, do proper family planning, properly invest and enlarge your streams of income so we can have enough to retire with so we will not have to work in our old age.

Benin proverb

One foot isn't enough to walk with.

No one will enjoy a half cooked meal no matter who makes it. One becomes valuable in his field when he has a reputation of integrity and hard work and perfection in projects.

As a career man, business man, student, athlete, friend, family man or whatever field one finds himself; one must endeavor to be a power house in it, you must be good and your works must be of good quality because once you are known for quality, kings and commoners will look for your services from many parts of the world.

Do not carry out your services dubiously and with the idea that no one is looking at you. Just offer a quality service and watch people overwhelm you with jobs.

South African proverb

The house fly that follows the meat seller never gets hungry

If you are a good student of African history or literature you will understand that our African ancestors were never people that derive joy in saying much, rather, just like the monks, they say little that has enough wisdom to fill pages just in paragraphs. In fact, there is an Igbo proverb that says that any man that asks for the interpretations to a proverb spoken to him is not man enough and that the dowry that was paid when his mother was married was a waste. I understand that the sensible thing to do for anyone in confusion is to ask questions. Yes, that is right but in Africa, there is a certain level of maturity you are expected to attain before you are seen as a man.

So with that being said, the proverb above is used to admonish the younger ones to be wise in choosing who they chose to learn from or partner with. It teaches that if you want to be a doctor, then it is right that you have an experienced doctor as a friend or mentor because he has definitely seen it all and although you are studying, there are still many things you will learn from him that school will not teach you. Same is applicable to other fields of life.

You need to work in the footsteps of a master so you
will not prolong your journey or fail.

Nigerian Proverb

"Our wife, our wife"; come midnight, we shall know whose wife she is.

Generally, this Malawian proverb is more of the use of humor to pass vital information. In most African settings, people, especially age grades and friends often refer to their friend's wives as 'our wife.' However, the proverb reminds everyone that come midnight, everyone will know the true husband of the woman. The message here is that sometimes one just has to remain calm and relax because something's are not worth worrying over because things will often times sort itself out.

Malawian proverb

The native doctor that told the sick widow to bring a virgin mosquito to cure her apparently has no plans to cure her.

This Angolan proverb teaches us the importance of being self-aware, smart, and streetwise so we do not rely or keep our hopes on people that don't want to render us any help or the people that are planning to defraud us.

The world is a scary place; it's not a place for the faint hearted and weak. To survive; just like adding a salt to a dish; you need to add some smartness and streetwiseness to your dealings with others. You should not trust blindly or believe the words of others because of their smiling faces or their bogus grammars and personality. Think about things thoroughly before you believe.

For reference purposes, the analogy for this proverb is derived from the fact that Africans are mostly traditionists and they normally consult their chief priests and native doctors to heal their ailments. While consulting, the native doctor's sometimes directs them to get some items to accelerate their healings. So for a native doctor to tell you to go and get a virgin mosquito, it indicates that he definitely has no plans of healing you.

Angolan proverb.

Only a fool tests the depth of a river with both feet's.

The game of life is a game that the weak and timid never survives. It is like an adventure game where cautiousness, calculated moves are very essential in surviving.

This proverb also teaches us not to be hasty in making life changing decisions. Never be in haste to marry, never be in haste to trust people, never be in a haste to make career decisions, never be in haste to invest, never be in haste in life to make any sort of important decision in your life. You need to think, weigh your options, plan and then execute properly. Never put all your eggs in one basket.

Kenyan proverb

Wealth is like a garden, if it is not properly cultivated, it will not yield good harvest.

I believe you have come across articles about people who later became poor after winning millions of dollars in lottery. Well, there is a reason for that and the reason is because they refused to water their garden. By garden, I mean, they refused to get financial education or employ someone with such backgrounds to invest, and get the money multiplying for them instead of trying to buy all the petty things they never had and blowing it away in luxuries, models and extravagant lifestyle.

You might think it will never be you but the truth remains that it is something that can happen to anyone without the necessary financial knowledge of making and saving money.

Resist extravagancy, impulsive buying, and questionable circle of friends, womanizing, and love of flashy and trendy things. Devote your time and resources on how to maintain and multiply the little you have because wealth runs away from a person without financial discipline.

Congolese proverb

Restless feet may walk you into a pit of vipers.

This proverb teaches us about the importance of guarding our tongues and utterances lest they put us in trouble or destroy other people's life.

It also teaches us to watch our steps in terms of who we associate with, where we follow them to, who we follow, our peers and things we do in life lest we walk into our own doom.

Nigerian proverb

No short road exists to get to the top of Mount Kilimanjaro.

There is a defined path for greatness in life. The routes might slightly differ but the outcome is normally the same.

To be a doctor, it is expected that you need to study, practice, learn even more, work hard with studies, pass your exams, and qualify before you become one. Such is also applied in athletics, engineering, architecture, arts, acting and others. You just need to do the needful and it is also no secret that you become better when you meticulously do the needful.

So, abhor laziness, procrastination, complacency and implore hard work, consistency, and tenacity so that you can achieve your dreams.

Kenyan proverb

When two mighty elephants tussle, it is the grass that bears the destruction.

We must not be selfish enough to think that everything revolves around us and that we forget that some of our actions will have consequences on the life of people around us. This is especially to parents, leaders and people with political powers.

Rwandan proverb

All monkeys cannot hang on the same branch.

Life's opportunities are so many for anyone to give up in life because he failed in one particular venture or career he embarked on. There are literally many things or so many ways to succeed that we mustn't relent if one fails.

Also, this proverb teaches that we mustn't be so myopic in dreaming and aiming that we must only succeed by doing what everyone around you is doing.

This is 21st century, so you can basically migrate to a safe new country, study and understand the problems they have that you can solve and earn from.

Move around, expand your horizon, learn more, travel more and never be afraid to go South when everyone is going West.

Burundi proverb

To try severally and fail is never laziness.

This proverb is used to encourage people that are facing hard times despite their efforts to succeed. The proverb understands that some people could be so unfortunate that they could work harder than every other person in the room and still be unsuccessful in the things they are doing. So this proverb is used to tell these people that they are never alone, that people see their efforts despite their misfortunes. It is also used to suggest to them that they should maybe look to explore other things.

Ghanaian proverb

A feeble effort will never satisfy self.

This proverb teaches us that a little effort or push in life only yields little or no significant result. Little work or dedication will only produce little or no significant result.

If you desire greatness or big results in whatever you are doing in life; the ideal thing to do is to put in the maximum required efforts and watch yourself actualize your dreams.

Egyptian proverb

An Iroko tree that has tasted fire will light up at the slightest touch with another fire.

This proverb is simply talking about how it is easy for someone who has been preparing for opportunities to grab those opportunities and succeed.

This is talking about the importance of one preparing himself ahead of time in readiness for any opportunity that lies ahead. Hence, the proverb implores us all to not to be so comfortable and complacent in life that we forget to get more knowledge to expand our knowledge in preparation of more opportunities in life.

Nigerian proverb

You must not call for a dog with a whip in your hand.

We need to take a break and look within ourselves sometimes to determine what is going wrong. We may unknowingly create situations which affects our growth sometimes and lay the blames on others.

You cannot have a whip in your hand and be calling a dog to come to you when they know what the whip is used for.

Look inward and find that which is delaying your progress or chasing away opportunities or valuable people from you and make the necessary adjustments.

Tanzanian proverb

There is never a time that rain only falls only on the roof of one person.

Life is never interested in you personally. You are not too important or to useless to her. You make or break yourself by the decisions you make in life. So, you must not be in haste to blame bad luck or the Almighty when life is not going your way.

It is not about you and the world never revolves around you.

Congolese proverb

No man born of a woman is born great; great people are born in the night when others sleep.

This proverb tries to warn us about the dangers of comparing ourselves with people that are born with silver spoon that seem to be doing well. The proverb tries to tell us that although these people are lucky enough, still they put in some hard work to make their selves better too.

Never relent from chasing your dreams by blaming bad government and lack of jobs, bad economy, limitations, disability, environment and hard luck. Instead, you have to go out there and fight for your destiny and do not keep wasting your life by blaming government and people.

Kenyan proverb

Marry a pig for his wealth, one day, the wealth will g but the pig remains.

Look beyond materiel things and selfish interests while getting into any sort of relationship with people. Do not marry a woman or man because of pretty face and body or wealth; rather look for character, compatibility, love, tolerance, kindness and humility. This is necessary because a person that possesses these qualities will be there for you and whatever you share with the person will last the test of time. And moreover, you will be treated with respect and love rather disgust.

Congolese proverb

If love lives in your house, darkness will flee.

The deep wisdom in this ancient proverb transcends beyond family and the concept of love among siblings. The house is only an analogy which represents the mind and soul of a human. It teaches us that once we are filled with love, compassion, empathy, gratitude, and kindness; we become light which everyone will want to identify with.

Egyptian proverb

When a youth is in love, a lion becomes a cat in his eyes.

This proverb is used to counsel parents and guardians to be very careful and try to do their best in giving their young ones the necessary advice when they start falling in love. This is necessary because the two inexperienced heads needs the input of an experienced head to make them know if it is truly love or they are being abused, taking advantage of, messing around the very worst kind of people. So watch your young ones to avoid regrets.

Zambian proverb

If she loves you, she will love you with your dirt's and smell.

Love is unconditional; it doesn't often come with clauses. So, this proverb is used to teach aspiring couples that what they are about to enter is a union of two souls that have now become one and shares each other's pains, joy, burdens and happiness. Once this union is formed, the goal becomes one and interests align and no one looks for theirs alone but for the collective good of the union. The proverb teaches people to be meticulous in whom they allow to use Love as a disguise to manipulate and take advantage of their naivety or innocence.

Be careful so you can differentiate between infatuations, lusts, psychological manipulations and true love.

Nigerian proverb

My son, never you become so attached and in love with someone that you cannot tell when it's raining.

Always learn how to apply restraints on how you show someone you are in love or like staying with them.

Do not allow someone to perceive desperation in your attempts to express your love or fondness for them. This proverb is used to teach people that there are possibilities of getting into the hands of a manipulator or opportunist that will use the opportunity to mess you up.

Zimbabwean proverb

Around a beautiful flower lurk many insects and weeds.

The great things in life don't just lay on a platter for anyone to grab. No, the great things of life often hide behind hard work, commitment, dedication, passion and consistency. This is the sweetness of life. We must not all be great. Greatness is left for those with the passion, commitment, dedication and consistency to dig in deep and get to it.

Life generally has no sympathy for the weak or naïve. You must have what it takes to succeed. Have you tried asking yourself why an ordinary person gets lucky and wins millions of dollars in lottery and loses all within a while? Well, it is because they didn't work hard to earn it so they don't know the value of what they have and have no respect for it so within a while it goes away.

Go out today and get busy, soil your hands if necessary, dirty your linen if necessary, lose sleep if necessary but endeavor to make sure you find a way to succeed.

Ugandan proverb

Lonely means one.

Life was never planned to be lived alone. We all need a soul that connects with us. We all need our own person that loves us unconditionally, wants the best for us, will be there under rain and sun for us. This person must not be a romantic partner; it could be a friend, a sibling, child, colleague or mentor.

Life its self is tough. So, why will anyone want to go through its tough terrains alone.

Pets, wealth, and career are not human, they have no soul and they could vanish one day but the human bond, psychological and emotional support that comes from it usually lasts the test of time.

So, open yourself to the possibility of quality bonding with others.

Egyptian proverb

**The young man with too much ambition
never sleeps well at night.**

This proverb is used to teach people that comfort and
complacency is a great enemy of progress. One must
not relent in his journey for greatness, laziness and
complacency will kill dreams more than any other
thing.

Pay the price needed for anything you want. Do not
look for shortcuts, go all in and do the needful.

Cameroun proverb

A fully grown Iroko tree cannot be bent to a walking stick.

Prepare your mind, body and soul so that the trials and tribulations of this life will not bend you over.

This proverb is used to remind people about the importance of mental toughness and general readiness for whatever life throws at us. Because, believe me, life will shake us up in her own way someday. It could come through the loss of a loved one, heartbreak, depression, sickness, insolvency and bad investments, hard luck and other misfortunes.

Toughen yourself up, do the best you can do for yourself and let the Almighty God take care of the things you can't change in life.

Nigerian proverb

One camel doesn't make fun of other camel's hump.

We are all human. We had no input on who gives birth to us, the religion we are born into, our background, our race, wholeness of our body and more. We just happen to find ourselves where we are. So if you are born with a silver spoon, you need to be empathetic, kind, compassionate and helpful to those that didn't have the same privilege you have. Do not look down on others because of their struggles in life. Do not think them as lazy or peasants. They too are humans like you.

Algerian proverb

The elephant doesn't limp even while walking on thorns.

Know when to show your weaknesses and know who you share your trials with. Yes, it is sometimes good to free yourself of some burdens by sharing your issues to people. However, this proverb is used to teach us not to be so open to people because the human mind is tricky, hence, people whom you trust today could change to your enemies tomorrow and use your weaknesses against you.

Rwandan proverb

No matter how fully grown the water is, it still wants more water.

The pocket of an ambitious man is never filled to his satisfaction. Work hard, learn more, research more, travel more, befriend more, merry more, do more adventurous activities and satisfy the urge of adventure and more which every human shares lest we die with regrets of not doing more on our death bed.

Tanzanian proverb

Good music goes with good laughter and food.

Traditionally, ancient Africans and Indians share some similarities with borders around the idea of merriment and good time with people of their kindred and families. Our ancestors understood the importance of breaking bread and drinking wine with good music in the company of our loved ones, hence, they use this proverb to admonish us to live in peace with our kinsmen, friends and families.

South African proverb

Birds of different feathers and whistling will end up perching on the same Iroko tree.

Find your tribe, find those that share similar values, affiliations, goals, and sentiments with you and align yourself so your journey in life will be made easier and you will have proper motivation to continue.

It is better to walk in union of likeminded people than to isolate yourself from family, real friends and people that share similar values with you.

Mozambique proverb

Sticks that are properly tied as a bundle are not easily broken.

This Tanzanian proverb teaches the importance of cohesion in life. It teaches that there is strength in unity and it is a vital element in achieving greatness in life.

It also teaches the importance of friendship with like-minded individuals and the importance of family.

Tanzanian proverb

The person, who earns calamity, will eat it with the family.

This proverb teaches us about the importance of strong family institutions because it remains the bedrock of the society. It also teaches the importance of parents being intentional in raising well behaved and ambitious children that are patriotic and ready to make their own impact in the society at large.

With the societal and moral decadence that is going on in America and most European countries; we need to go back to some of the traditional ways that had always worked for us because of the impact that good family institutions had for us at large.

We should go back to our drawing board and check where we are getting it wrong and make the necessary adjustments and tone it down on the Wokeness and delusions.

Zambian proverb

It takes the whole community to raise a good child.

Good and strong family institutions that are properly mixed with communal care where elderly people in one way or the other looks out for the young ones and helps the parents to raise responsible and patriotic children.

This proverb is used to inform people that raising children is not only the job of the parents, however, it is a role which people should directly or indirectly involve their selves because responsible and patriotic children is a good thing for the society at large.

Nigerian proverb

A small cubicle will make a home for ten good friends.

Life is much more than selfish interests, wealth and influence. Nothing beats the feelings of being surrounded by people, whether family, colleagues or mates who wants only the best for you and shares similar goals with you.

Be at peace with your family, love and cherish them. Build stronger bonds with people who love you and know that life gets easier with these people than isolating yourself for the pursuant of career and wealth. I am not implying that going after your career is not necessary. No, I am simply implying that there should be a proper balance of the two.

Zimbabwean proverb

It is not bad to dine with a stranger; however, it is vital that you save your love for family.

We can select our friends but family is just part of us. Yes, some families are toxic but we must by all means be pillars for each member; hence this proverb is used to teach people to honor their family and always put them first before strangers. However, it is vital that we find a way to separate family from business if you doubt their ability to play a significant role in growing it.

Liberia proverb

One who plants apple by the roadside has similar problems with one who married beautiful that has no discipline.

This proverb is about the importance of doing a thorough background check of the person we wish to marry.

The proverb teaches people to look beyond beauty, handsomeness, curvy body and riches when they want to marry and first know the type of family they are marrying into, the partner's past life, upbringing and beliefs lest they marry who they don't know.

Burundi proverb

A home without a good woman is like a zoo without animals.

This proverb is used to teach the importance of cultured and good women in every home, community, and society. As the man has his own roles to play in the family and society at large, so does the woman have her own important roles to play in the family and society too. None is more important than another; it's all about everyone playing their role for the greater good.

Zambian proverb

The Nile alligator and the hawk might fall in love, but the two cannot build a home.

Marriage is not all about love. There are other factors that determine the foundation of a good marriage. These factors range from compatibility, tolerance, kindness, compassion, sympathy, like-mindedness, shared goals and interests. Without these things, love will fade away and lovers will turn strangers.

According to the lesson in this proverb; it is vital that aspiring couples looks beyond their amateur feelings and be very certain that they are not feeling lust, infatuations or confused when they are choosing partners. It also teaches that these aspiring couples must look deep to ascertain if they have those factors listed above before getting into marriage.

Egyptian proverb

The unwise speaks; the wise listens.

There is a reason every person has two ears and one mouth. You need to listen twice and only speak little on what you know what to talk about. Speak only when you have something important to say. Listen twice, hear from both parties, and do not be in a haste to speak.

Moroccan proverb

Yes, they love each other but they have long noses; now, tell me, how can they kiss?

If you are a good student of African literature you will understand that marriage and the concept of family has been an important aspect of the ancient African societies. You are in fact considered not man or woman enough if you your golden age passes you without you being married. It is in fact a crime that brings about many dehumanizing treatments from even your own family. So, getting married was a major achievement back then, even till now in most African societies. However, divorce was frowned upon then, even till now in most African customs. Marriage was seen as a permanent union of two people.

So, marriage being something that ought to last forever; our ancestors used this proverb to admonish the aspiring couples then to take their time and look for who they are compatible with, who they can tolerate their excesses, who they think suits them better than simply going for love or what they have to gain from the person. Same is applicable to us today. Look for compatibility, kindness, compassion, empathy, tolerance, shared interests and goals in the person you plan to live out your life with.

Egyptian proverb

Yes, you know who you love but you don't know who loves you.

This particular proverb teaches us the importance of understanding that we should take out time and exercise caution and patience in selecting who we chose to call friends or lovers. It is not everyone that is blessed with discerning spirit to see through people's gimmicks and masks. So, it is wise that we do our own home work in our own way to ascertain the true intentions of who we chose to spend the rest of our lives with.

Ivory Coast proverb

If a beautiful lady doesn't love you, she will call you her brother.

Pay attention to the silent things that people around you are saying. The heart of a person is tricky in nature. So, it is wise that you pay maximum attention to those slight expressions the body shows. Do not overlook red flags in people and lovers when you see them. Try to understand who needs you for the benefits they can get from you and not who needs you for who you truly are. Never downplay the toxicity of people who keeps promising to change. Believe me, that change will never come and they will so pummel you into you psychologically surrender and take their toxicity as normal.

Ghana proverb

Knowledge and wisdom is like fire. People take it from others.

This proverb teaches about the importance of mentorship and apprenticeship in transferring knowledge from generation to generation.

Just like the popular Igbo apprenticeship where traders bring young ones from the village to teach them the trade and also support them with cash after their apprenticeship with him. Doing this have helped pull many families out of poverty and have also helped grow the GDP of Nigeria at large.

Another type of this transfer of knowledge is the act whereby old and experienced heads in many fields of work picks newbies under their wings and helps them get better. This is also seen in academics where lecturers or professors or even teachers and coaches takes students under their watchful eyes and helps them focus more and study.

In summary, newbies should endeavor to identify with old heads that will put them through in life. This is applicable to athletes, students, career people, young couple and every other person.

Nigerian proverb

To get lost is to learn the right path.

There is no harm in trying in life. The harm is actually in not trying. Not getting up from your comfort zone, excuses, procrastinations, limitations and going after your aspirations.

There is no better teacher in life than experience, and the experience will come from you trying. You need to take calculated risks in life. Don't worry if you fail at the first time of trying. Try again; at least you are coming with experience which will help you not to repeat those things that made you fail. Instead you will try new methods, hence not repeating the initial mistakes.

Ethiopian proverb

The council's wisdom prevents the great king from being called a fool.

Wisdom is always profitable for they that knows its value and seeks it.

It is almost certain that there is no one that is an expert in everything in life. You can't know it all; there must be limitations to your knowledge in life. You could be a good scientist and still be a terrible accountant or chef. You could be a good mathematician and still be a terrible poet. You could be a professor of literature and still be terrible in economics. This is understandable. We can't know it all. Where your knowledge stops is where another person's own starts. With these above facts; this proverb tries to teach us understand our weakness and find means to surround ourselves with people who their strengths compliments ours.

A good leader should know that he doesn't know everything and is thus expected to find people that are good in those areas he lacks and surrounds himself with such people. Do not allow pride and ignorance to think you know everything and move in such manner. It will only be a step to your downfall.

Ethiopian proverb

My son, you must be vigilant because just because the Agama lizard nodded his head before leaving doesn't mean he is in agreement with you.

Do not live your life and deal with people based on your assumptions and feelings. Be careful not to rely on your predictions about the behaviors of others.

Be very certain about things before you begin to draw conclusions about them.

Nigerian proverb

A fool always has to say something. The wise has something to say.

Don't be the talkative in the room, be the silent one that only speaks up when he truly has something vital to say.

No wise person takes a talkative serious. No one feels comfortable discussing sensitive issues with them in the room.

Always speak with empirical facts so you will not contradict your words tomorrow or make a fool of yourself.

Congolese proverb

A woman's destruction lies in her tongue.

This proverb is not just about women; the proverb is for both genders and it is used to warn people to be very careful of their utterances, especially while angry.

Some words are so cruel that once they come out, they can never be taken back and the wounds they make never heal.

Mind your utterances, talk less, and only talk when you have something important to talk about. Refrain from gossips, blackmail, and unfounded criticism and verbal attacks and online trolling.

Zambian proverb

The man who doesn't know one thing definitely knows another.

Do not be quick to write people off in life. No one is completely useless in life. Treat people with respect and compassion in life because they might be the one to help you with something you don't know or have tomorrow.

Tanzanian proverb

If you are in peace with your family, you are a successful person.

There are many things that matters in life than your career, wealth and the quest for money. One of those things is family.

Family is one of the things that makes life worth living most times. Is it not just lovely that there are people that share the same blood with you, people who nursed you to adulthood, people that love you unconditionally, and people that are there for you no matter the season or the condition? Yes, they might be annoying sometimes, but deep inside you, you know they love you to death. That is what love is like. That is what you should never place career or ambitions over. You must balance them and other things.

If you are at loggerheads with yours, find way to make peace and reconcile.

Also, endeavor to build your own. Get yourself a good partner, build a home together and enjoy yourself by watching your seeds grow.

South African proverbs

One who loves a pot must also love what is inside it.

Stay and never leave the place where you are appreciated for who you are. Be careful around those whose love for you is just conditional. Be wary around people that only come around you when they need you to do something for them. That is not love; it is just a parasitic and manipulative relationship which you must leave.

Someone who loves you usually loves you with your dirt. They will love you with it first and if the dirt is much, they will help you get clean.

Kenyan proverb

When you show a fool the moon the fool sees only your finger.

Be careful not to surround yourself with less ambitious characters that will never help you grow because they are too daft to recognize opportunities or compliment on your weaknesses and make you stronger.

Also, do not waste your precious time trying to better an ignorant fellow that has no interest in being successful in life. Leave such characters less they drag you down to their mud of ignorance. Let ignorance teach them a lesson.

Ethiopian proverb

Even the drunkard has a family.

Everyone is loved somewhere and they mean a lot to some people somewhere. Do not underrate or belittle people in life because you feel they are nothing and insignificant.

Treat everyone with respect and compassion because just like you, they too are humans and has emotions as well.

Tanzanian proverb

The foolish housefly without a counselor follows the corps to the grave.

One must endeavor to have capable and experienced heads that will help them go through life's rough terrains without getting stuck.

This great Nigerian proverb teaches us the importance of having experienced people to advise us in the things we plan to do in life. The proverb teaches that it is not just about having them around, it teaches that we also need to pay attention to their wise words lest we do the same mistakes that they did in life.

The analogy of this proverb is derived from the fact that ancient Africans didn't really bury their dead in a closed casket, their dead where mostly wrapped in clothes or mats, so they were exposed to houseflies. Hence, the proverb is saying that any housefly that doesn't have anyone to tell it not to follow the dead to the grave will be buried with the dead.

Nigerian proverb

If you arrive at a place where people cut of their ears, it is expected that you cut of yours too and do as others are doing.

Life is not always about you alone. We must endeavor to live a community life where everyone tries to directly or indirectly help to better the lives of others too.

This Zimbabwean proverb teaches the importance of living an impactful life. It teaches us to respect others and their culture, religion and preferences. This proverb teaches tolerance.

Zimbabwean proverb

The toad doesn't run in the afternoon in vain. It is either it is chasing something or something is after it.

This Nigerian proverb teaches us the importance of self and environmental awareness. The proverb is a very popular one in the Eastern region of Nigeria which is mostly used by someone who is going through tough times or challenges and comes to his friend, family or tribesman for help. The proverb is usually implored to inform someone that the situation is bad even without saying what the actual situation is.

The analogy is derived from the fact that toads are usually nighttime animal. They are not known for operating in day time, so it is assumed that once you see one running about in the day time, it is either something is after it or it is after something.

Nigerian proverb

My son, hear me. He who goes to the river to fish without fishing net and hooks is only going to the river to take his bath.

Proper knowledge and understanding of whatever one is doing in life with preparedness and readiness are vital components of success for every aspiring professional.

This lovely proverb teaches that one must have their tools for that which they seek to do in life. An athlete needs to prepare for the big arenas by being the hardest worker on the turf, he must train more than others, he must live according to a proper diet, and he must have proper sleep and lifestyle so he can perform when called upon. Such is applicable to other fields. If you want to be a programmer, then you must commit yourself, time, and resources to learning for years. So the commitment of your time, energy, resources are your fishing nets and hook here of which failing to get them simply means that you will never be the programmer you wished to be. So get your essential tools ready and move for that which you aspire to be. There is no shortcut in life.

Egyptian Proverb

No matter how the he goat frowns, it will still be taken to the market.

What will be will be. This proverb admonishes us about the concept of staying away from procrastination or the fear of the eventualities of life. It teaches that it is okay to be scared, anxious, and nervous sometimes about things in life. However, we shouldn't dwell too much on these emotions as they are simply the things that make us human. We, as humans needs to understand that we will one day lose our parents, partners, friends, colleagues, and possibly children to the cold hand of death. We need to understand that trials and tribulations of all kinds and sickness or misfortunes is a natural occurrences that can happen to anyone no matter how hard one tries to avoid them. So this proverb teaches that one should take it all with grace and know that it is just what it is. This is how life works.

Nigerian proverb

My son, what you will be in the future is carefully intertwined in your daily habits.

It is no secret that we eventually become what we spend our time doing. This Tanzanian proverb is teaching us that there is always footprints of what we spend most of our youthful times on when we eventually get old. You can't spend your productive years drinking recklessly, womanizing, smoking, partying away your time and sleeping and expect to have an early and comfortable retirement when you get old.

You must take full advantage of the strength and capacity that you are blessed with as a youth to clear a part for your future. You must consistently study, practice, develop yourself the furthest you can in the field that you want so that you can be the best and make yourself valuable.

Tanzanian proverb

One cannot carry two Nile watermelons in one hand.

This Egyptian proverb teaches the importance of priorities. It teaches the importance of one going after his priorities than chasing many things at a time and losing all because you didn't focus on one.

We, as a people must learn how to plan, understand things in perspectives and how important they are and give each one attention based on their relevance.

This wise proverb is derived from the fact that the Egyptian watermelons that are planted around the river Nile are often very big; hence, it is practically impossible to carry two with one hand.

Egyptian proverb

An old woman doesn't get old in the song she used to dance while she was young.

This Ethiopian proverb teaches us about the importance of hard work, consistency and dedicating for anyone in whichever field they so desire. According to the proverb; if you consistently dedicate your time, resources in learning and perfecting your skills in any field. It is certain that you will become so good at it that you will be valued more than your colleagues and the rewards will come and you will see yourself going places and dining with CEOs and MDs.

So, get your lazy bums up and go and perfect that which you are doing. Outwork everyone in the room. Be the best at whatever you are doing so you will be known as a rock in that field.

Ethiopian proverb

**You are expected to eat only when the food
is ready; you are also expected to speak
only when you have something to say and
the time is right.**

Say something when you are certain you have
something important to say. Do not be quick to utter
things you are not sure of or say more than needed.

Bridle your tongue lest you say much today and
contradict yourself tomorrow.

Ethiopian proverb

He who has no patience can never make a beer.

Life is a journey that requires patience to go through it. Never be in a haste to make decisions about anything in your life. Do not be quick to draw conclusions on people and situations.

Nothing comes easy in life. Just do the needful and apply patience and with time it will all make sense.

Congolese proverb

He who always tells the truth is never wrong in the eyes of the kinsmen.

This particular proverb is used to teach people that people around them often time judges them by what they are known for. It teaches about the importance of being responsible and honest so much that people know you and become eager to vouch for you in your absence.

If people know you as the honest one, the responsible, and kind and compassionate; they will always have that side of you in their mind and will protect your interests even in rooms that you are not present.

Kenyan proverb

Where water is the king, there the land must obey.

This proverb teaches about the importance of environmental awareness, respect, service and humility in whatever we do in life.

Africa is a land of kings and queens. Every piece of land or community has their own leader and it is expected that the absolute respect is accorded to these entities because they are the custodians of the law and overseer of our communities.

In the context of this proverb, these entities can be your parents, elder siblings, partners, senior colleagues, mates, friends, mentors, teachers, and people in authority. Give respect to whom it is due.

Algerian proverb

The little bird cannot crow until it hears the older ones crow.

This particular proverb is used to teach parents, guardians, elders and teachers that they are the indirect role models of the young ones around them. These cute ones see everything you do, they learn, and they will one day practice the things they have learnt from you. So it is very important that people know this and apply caution on what they say, do and practice around the young ones because they will surely mimic you tomorrow.

Congolese proverb

The child of a rat is a rat.

History matters unless there is a beyond doubt prove to indicate a different pattern.

This proverb tries to teach people to try and have background knowledge of the people they are dealing with, especially in a relationship and business. Pay good attention to people's past because it often has a way of repeating itself in the future.

Humans are practically predictable character wise and they tend to be repetitive in this regard. So pay attention to the past of the people around you and apply the necessary cautions.

Kenyan proverb

Do a good deed and let the crickets of the night never hear of it.

This sweet proverb has become so relevant in this our time where people uses their left hand to hand out help and uses their right hand to snap and upload it online for likes and recognition.

It is very unkind for you to use the faces of the needy to seek personal aggrandizement among your peers and strangers online. Offer help if you can but resist that silly urge of seeking personal glory with it by showing people what you just did. It is not necessary because although those people smile into your cameras, they really don't want you to show them in their vulnerabilities and lowest state.

Somalia proverb.

If your only tool is a hammer, you will see every problem as a nail.

There are always different perspectives to things. A simple period of thinking or consultation of relevant people in any problem will bring forth different approaches of solving whatever the issue is. Do not be so ignorantly strong headed that you assume you know everything and do not need the input of others. Hence, this proverb teaches about the importance of broadening one's view, horizon and perspective by being open to people's inputs, studies, researches, and corrections.

Sudanese proverb

A child is the child of everyone in community.

This Sudanese proverb teaches that raising a child is not only the duty of the parents. In as much as there are boundaries to the length you can associate yourself with other people's children, it is still expected that an elderly plays their role in helping to raise up responsible and patriotic children. No elderly person should seat still and watch a child put his hands in fire. It is expected that you should caution them or talk to their parents about their child's misdeeds. Play your role.

Sudanese proverb

Be a mountain or find one to lean on.

This great Somalia proverb teaches the importance of one finding his tribe, his soul mate, his support and rock to lean on when things start getting confusing in life.

The essence of this great proverb borders around the fact that we all as humans needs one another to be able to navigate life properly. You need me, I need you. No one is an island. UBUNTU! I am because you are.

Somali proverb.

An orphaned calf licks its own back.

Life doesn't care about your limitations, disability, poor background, religion, race, political affiliations and feelings. No one has got your back except you. You need to wake up and go after your dreams and stop clouding your laziness, low ambition and uselessness under the guise of disability, race card, poor background and any other excuse you can think of.

Go after your dreams now and forget about your excuses. No one is coming to rescue you from mediocrity and poverty. You are the only one that can save yourself.

Kenyan proverb

It is by crawling that a child knows how to stand and walk.

Life is a stage by stage journey. One must not miss the necessary steps required to take him to the next stage. You can't just try to jump over steps to hasten your journey. You have to follow the steps so that you will not jump into your own downfall.

A child must crawl first, then the child will learn to stand and from there the child will start walking. That is just the simple rule of life.

Pay the necessary dues required to make you great in life. Do not allow distractions and laziness make you jump steps without familiarizing yourself in each step you have taken.

To be a doctor, you must study hard, do researches, do practicals, learn more and pass your tests and examinations before you are certified to practice. Apply this to other areas of life and you will understand better that those prices must be duly paid before glory comes.

Malian proverb

If you close your eyes to the truth, you will learn through misfortunes.

There is no deceit bigger than one deceiving himself.
You need to look at yourself in the mirror and tell the
person you see on the mirror the very simple truth.
You need to advice yourself today. Look at the way
your life is going, are you happy with it? What sort of
future does it hold for you? What can I do to better my
situation and progress?

You need to ask yourself those questions and honestly
answer them and immediately put into action
whatever you feel will remedy the situation.

If you are fat, that is because you eat too much. If you
fail exams, that is because you don't study well. Don't
deceive yourself again. Speak to yourself and make the
necessary adjustments today.

Ghana proverb

Rising early makes the road shorter.

Time and tide they say waits for no person regardless of the person's disability, background, limitations, race, religion, political affiliations or interests in life.

The race of life is one that is brutal, mean and rigorous. And the way to conquer it is to first start off early in life, be consistent and dedicated to your journey and never look back but forge ahead no matter the distractions that may come from behind.

Do not wait for things to get too late and make you start off in a haste and unprepared.

Togolese proverb

By the time the fool learns the game, the game must have finished and the players dispersed.

The game of life is one that has no rules for participants. The whistle was blown the day you were born. The game of life has no regards about your disadvantages, limitations, or your feelings.

You need to move fast, acquire the necessary skills, and knowledge you need to conquer and move.

There will be many injustices and people that will do all they can to unsettle you and get you out of the race; however, you must be focused to get the price which is success as you define it.

Ghana proverb

Do not allow your stomach to make you useless.

This very special proverb teaches the importance of self-discipline, integrity and the power of being contented with what you have. It teaches that it is not good for one to be so predictable and shameless that he can be lured into changing white to black with food or money.

Someone that is incorruptible is one that has already conquered greed and the appetite for things gotten from bribery and criminality.

The proverb teaches us that living a life of greed will make people see us dishonest characters that can be swayed by the sight of currency and other enticing things.

Kenyan proverb

When the mother goat breaks into the yam barn to steal yam, the kid watches her.

This particular proverb is mostly used to teach adults and parents about the importance of being careful about what they say or do in front of kids because they see you as a role model and they will replicate the things they see you doing or say the things they hear you saying.

Nigerian proverb

By trying often, the monkey learns how to jump from branch to another.

Experience is the best teacher one can get in life. Also, consistency in the face of failure builds one to be a force to be reckoned with in any field the person is.

We have to keep pushing in the face of failure, disappointments, betrayal and loss.

Do not be discouraged because the first trial didn't work. How about you keep on trying no matter how long you fail in that which you are certain is the right path and dream for you.

Never consider giving up for anything because there is a light at the very end of that tunnel for you.

Ugandan proverb

Maize bears fruits once and dies because its roots are not deep rooted in the ground.

Be very good at whatever you do so that little challenges will not blow you off your feet.

Dedicate enough time in learning and perfecting your craft. Doing this will give you all the knowledge you need about it and it will also help you become a go to person in it.

Nigerian proverb

Once a handshake passes the elbow its true intentions are questioned.

We need to be careful and vigilant to know when people are simply trying to take advantage of us or overstep their boundaries.

Place your boundaries. Be vocal and very arrogant about it lest people take advantage of you and see you as a fool

Nigerian proverb.

Avoid him who enjoys burial food but recovers once sickness visits him

This proverb talks about the importance of avoiding selfish characters that only wants to eat from other's money no matter the cost but will never bring out a cent from their pocket for those that spends a lot for them.

Nigerian proverb

The very thing that killed the mother chicken will lurk around to ensure that its chicks never see the sun again.

This proverb is used to teach people to pay good attention to some underlying patterns in their history or the history of people they deal with.

Life is full of many mysteries and some of them are beyond our understanding no matter how much we try to get a grasp of them.

Pay good attention to things that happen around you lest you be consumed by the same thing things that consumed those before you.

Nigerian proverb

If that rat cannot sprint fast enough let it make way for the tortoise.

This proverb teaches us to know when to sit back and watch others progress. It also teaches us to be kind enough to carry the newbies in our field under our wings so we can teach them the things we know and let them shine.

This Ghanaian proverb also teaches us that we shouldn't try to block or hinder others from success or glory simply because we feel we have authority or influence. The world doesn't revolve around you. It's a journey we are in, your time comes and goes and the next person takes charge. Don't try to hinder Mother Nature from her duties or she will teach you a lesson in life.

Ghana proverb

The day I need a wife is the day that the market becomes filled up with mad women.

This proverb is used by many to express their frustration especially when things are not going well for them or when they are feeling unlucky.

Cameroun proverb

He who sees the chicken using its feet to scatter excrement should stop it because no one knows who will eat the leg tomorrow.

This proverb is used to teach people to be selfless in their activities and always look out for the collective good of people sometimes rather than only their interests.

This proverb also teaches the importance of understanding that what goes around sometimes comes around. We shouldn't live a negligent life; we should live a communal life with the good of everyone in mind because the harm we saw and left on the road might befall our loved ones too.

Nigerian proverb

The child that his father sends to rob his neighbor breaks the door with his feet.

No one is completely useless in life. All you may need is just the right kick at your back or rather, the right motivation to unleash the genius in you. Find the right course or motivation within you to start off today.

As for triggers, loss, fear of poverty, heartbreaks, embarrassments, inability to afford your basics could help to push you to greatness. Search within yourself and you will find the motivation you need to push you to greatness today.

Nigerian proverb

No one makes a good tone by beating the drums with one finger.

There are no shortcuts to greatness in life. You must do the needful to attain any level of success you dream of.

Endeavor to fully understand what you are going into as a career, business, studies and lifestyle and fully commit yourself to bettering yourself in it every day so you can become a force that cannot be ignored once your services are needed.

South African proverb.

He who the gods wants to kill they first make mad.

This proverb teaches us to be watchful of the people we deal with because some are just loads of bad luck and misfortunes walking around.

In Africa, we are strong believers of the supernatural and Karma. We believe that one who soils his hands with murder, rape, fraud, and other crimes, especially the oppression of the weak will get the wrath of the gods. So, the elders use this proverb to warn people to know who they deal with lest they associate with such people and share in their bad luck.

Nigerian proverb

When two elephants meet on a narrow bridge, one must wait for the other to pass first or they will not pass.

Life is not all about aggression, hostility and hot headedness. No, it is not what is often needed in navigating the tricky and thorny paths of life. Common sense is not common again. That shouldn't be the case. We must learn to apply it in all we do. We must learn how to apply patience, understanding and wisdom in the way we do things in life.

There is due process that has to be acknowledged and adhered to.

Rwanda proverb

You don't expect to find a virgin in the maternity ward.

People past matters on how you deal with them in the future. Do not expect a fox to start eating grass. Yes, people do change for good sometimes but it is safer for you to deal with them meticulously lest they catch you unawares.

Do not expect too much from people. When you deal with people, you have to be cautious and think properly. Don't trust easily and do not be swayed by the eloquence and sweet tongue of the cunning man.

Zimbabwean proverb

One must not call where he lives a jungle.

This proverb teaches us the importance of cleanliness, the importance of appreciation and love for our immediate environment and Mother Nature.

As a grown up, nobody will take you serious if you appear dirty, smelly, unkempt and lousy every time. We need to be disciplined enough to always make our beds when we wake, keep our environment neat, keep our self very neat and live as humans and not animals.

The proverb also teaches us to be grateful for our current situation and never undermine those that are helping us with the little they have when we have nothing.

Congolese proverb

One must not set sail using another person's star.

No one goes through life for another person. It is an individual matter. You get to carry your cross by yourself. You get to put in the required efforts needed for your success by yourself. Yes, your parents, partner or friend might be wealthy and influential enough to soften your paths but their influence can only last for a while.

The proverb also teaches us to try to take our own destiny by our hands instead of basing our own life and struggles by other's experiences. You mustn't assume you cannot be great in life just because no one in your family or region has attained such position in life. You just need to believe in yourself, put in the required efforts consistently and watch yourself become that you have always dreamed about.

Egyptian proverb

If life beats you up and gives you swollen face, just smile and act like one with a fat face.

This proverb is very deep in meaning that makes it one of my favorite Libyan proverbs. The proverb is used to teach people to keep their heads up and hold life and its troubles by the horn and move and find a way to survive regardless of how many times life beats them down.

Life is never a bed of roses. Believe me, it is full of thorns. Some get lucky enough to navigate it with fewer challenges while others have to conquer many trials to succeed. However, what actually matters is that we all should understand that it sometimes gets thorny. So, we must endeavor to fight like lions until we get what we want out of life.

Libyan proverb

He who begs his gods for rain also begs them for mud and mosquitoes.

This great Niger proverb teaches us to be careful of what we wish for or fight for.

Sometimes what we desire and fight for usually come with their problems as well.

He who wishes for wealth must have the heart to fight envy, hatred, and jealousy, threat to life and property and manipulations.

He who wishes to set a new world record in athletics should be ready for the grueling exercise, lonely lifestyle and sacrifices needed.

Niger proverb

**Send the lazy child to the playing ground
and you will see he is not really lazy.**

This proverb teaches us to be meticulous in
understanding the weaknesses and strengths of those
we work with, study with, siblings and friends so we
can know how to best maximize their potentials.

Everyone is a genius at something, however, what most
needs is just someone to help them see their strength
and maximize it.

Togolese proverb

The river never swallows the child whose legs it did not come in contact with.

This South African proverb teaches us that trouble doesn't necessarily come looking for those that avoid it. It also teaches us that success and greatness doesn't just come to those that are not ready to put in the work.

To be a medical doctor, it is expected that you must dedicate a sizeable number of years plus hard work, serious studies, research, practical's and consistency for you to be certified as one. You don't just attain greatness or your heart desires by mere and wishful fantasies. You need to come in contact with the river which in this context stands for hard work and dedication needed to excel.

South African proverb.

Yes my son; being hasty can make you few purses of coins but being patient will make you bags of coins.

This Gambian proverb teaches us about the importance of patience and proper strategy in whatever we are doing in life.

According to the proverb's interpretation, a fool is only worried about satisfying his tummy for the hour without thinking about the future.

Be it in academics, career, work, relationships and in all our dealings with others, we need to understand that the world will not end today, hence we should treat whatever we are doing with the idea that there is always tomorrow. So save money today so that it can save you tomorrow. Eat healthy in your early days so you can live a healthy life. Work hard now and get money so you can retire early and not waste your late ages working for people.

Gambian proverb.

The vulture and the Eagle do not struggle for food; the vulture is a scavenger, and the eagle is a predator.

There is this saying in most African region about one knowing who they are and what they truly represent in their community. To explain better; this proverb is used to remind the young and the old that they must know their worth, status, responsibility, what is expected of them and the family they are from and try to live accordingly.

To use myself to explain, I grew up in a Christian home. My dad was an Anglican priest before he retired. So to keep I and my siblings in check, he will always admonish us to live an exemplary life and try not to associate with the bad apples in our age grade. Yes, it might sound classist but he was just trying to let us understand that we should live a life worth emulating for other kids. So in essence, the eagle and the vulture can't struggle for food because they don't eat the same thing.

Nigerian proverb.

While on top of the Iroko tree, one must gather all the firewood he can because it is not every day that one gets to climb an Iroko three.

Endeavor to take full advantage of every opportunity that is presented to you because you never can tell if you will be opportune to see such opportunities in life again. This is basically what this proverb is saying.

The analogy is derived from the fact that the Iroko tree is a very tall and mighty tree that is sacred in most African regions and you don't just see people on it that often, so the proverb is saying, if you eventually get to the top, which is rare, you should use that opportunity and cut all the firewood you can because you might not be able to cut it tomorrow.

Cameroun proverb.

The sheep that desires to grow horns should first ask the ram how it carries its own horns.

This proverb teaches that there is always a price to pay for every great thing. Big achievers don't just get their success from wishful thinking, no; they put in the required hard work and consistency required.

This proverb also teaches the importance of proper consultations of people that have succeeded in whatever it is that you desire to do in life. It is vital that you hear from such sages so they will help you plant your feet properly so you will not make the same mistakes they made or waste your time in things that could have been achieved sooner.

South Sudan proverb.

Who will know more of the evils of witchcraft than the widow who lost her only child to evil spirits?

Always go to the right source for the information you seek in life. If you are sick, you are expected to see a medical practitioner. If you need to build a house you need to hire construction workers. If you want to be a doctor you need to go to medical school, consult highly trained lecturers and professors to be a good doctor. If you want to be a good musician you need to consult good producers and DJs. Always go to the right source for the information and skills you need.

Ugandan proverb.

The hunter who is bringing home the carcass of the elephant he killed has no time to search for crickets with his legs.

Always endeavor to see the bigger pictures in whatever you are doing. Do not fall to chasing smaller dreams when the bigger dreams are there for the taking.

This great Botswana proverb is used to admonish people to always pay attention to the bigger and important things in life. It is also used to tell people not to be swayed by greed for things that will expose you to lose the important ones.

Botswana proverb.

You can't say that a market will be bad in the morning

This precious proverb tries to admonish us about the dangers of easy and hasty conclusions and judgments about people, business and every other thing in life.

The analogy to the proverb is derived from the fact that a trader who says that the day's market will be bad and full of loses in the morning is either drunk or doesn't really know what he is saying because it's just morning and consumers have not started coming yet so it can still turn out to be a very good market day by the evening.

So, as it all implies, patience and better calculated moves are vital in making better decisions in life.

Cameroun proverb

"May the child not die, may the child not die." Let him die and let's see if day will not break.

Certain things are simply beyond our control as humans. Sometimes we can only hope for the best while we pray that the Almighty God shows us grace.

This Niger proverb is used to tell people that the world doesn't revolve around anyone and that no matter how close to heart we hold someone or something that we will one day lose them and the world will still continue.

You will one day lose you mum, father, siblings, relatives, friends, pets, colleagues and money or they may even lose you but nothing like such loses will halt the natural projection of the world.

We lost Queen Elizabeth, Nelson Mandela, Michael Jackson, DMX, 2Pac, Whitney Houston, Mother Theresa, Pele, Maradona, Kobe, The Pope and other important figures and the world never ceased working in its natural state. Que, sera, sera.

Niger proverb.

The chicken is angry with the cooking pot, forgetting the knife that slit its throat.

This proverb teaches us to always be very meticulous in observing situations and people before we come to our own conclusions.

It also teaches us to not throw blames without understanding the actual situation.

Congolese proverb.

Every morning; a gazelle wakes up knowing it should out run all the lions if it wants to see the dawn of the day.

The world is a scary place that has no regards for your feelings, excuses, disabilities, background, race or religion. The rules are simple and are for everyone. It is a game that only the strong and hard workers survive and flourish in.

To survive, you must prepare all the tools you need to survive, acquire the necessary skills, plan and strategize, be passionate and dedicate your time, resources and energy towards implementing those plans. You must wake up every day and live it like it will be your very last day by going out there to make a name for yourself.

Kenyan proverb.

The house fly only follows him who has smelly carcass.

This Ivory Coast proverb is all about teaching the young ones that to be a leader, there are some characters and virtues that ought to qualify one for it and that also stands as what people needs to see to follow. If you want to be a leader, it is expected that people who you want to lead must believe and trust you, deem you worthy of fellowship and make themselves available for your directives. You must give them reason to follow you. As a man, you must give your wife and kids enough reason in your actions to trust you to be the man of the house. You simply do not get it from being violent.

The analogy of the proverb is derived from the fact that houseflies loves smelly things and they are ready to follow any carcass they come across to the ends of the earth. That also applies to us that desire to be leaders in any capacity; do you have the carcass that will attract fellowship?

Ivory Coast proverb.

The little masquerade is only powerful because the big masquerade is not outside yet.

No matter who you are or the type of wealth and power you have amassed, where your money stops is where another person's own begins.

This Rwandan proverb is used to admonish both the old and young about humility. You have to be humble in your dealings with everyone. You need to know that we are nothing but a bag of dust with a heart pumping blood and any day it stops, it ends.

Treat everyone with the utmost respect and empathy for this will earn you their respect than arrogance and pride.

Rwanda proverb.

Fire and gunpowder cannot marry.

Yes, love is necessary in any union, however, compatibility, tolerance, and kindness are major factors that must not be ignored for any reason. Hence, this proverb is simply used to teach aspiring couples to try and be sure that what they feel is not lust and infatuation for someone. It teaches us to take all the time we need to ensure that we are about to marry someone we are compatible with than simply going into unions because we just love the person.

This also applies to other partnerships which include, business venture partnership, career, studies, friendship and others. Be certain to know if you can actually work together or tolerate each other before you commit.

Liberian proverb

Rain beats the tiger but it never washes away its spots.

This Kenyan proverb is used to remind people how strong, special and successful they are and can be if they ignore trials of life and continue to push on in life.

The analogy of this proverb is gotten from the fact that tiger's spots are permanent and can never be washed away regardless of the rain that beats them. So, we all have the elements to survive and no matter the challenges we face in life, these elements will not be conquered once we are willing to push through and succeed.

Kenyan proverb

It is always the calm and still water that drowns a man.

This proverb is so important that it is so popular in Congo and bordering countries.

It is all about one being very careful in downplaying things or underestimating problems, tasks, and opportunities in life.

Crocodiles normally hide in calm waters waiting for their prey. Calm waters often have serious muds underneath it that traps animals and men that dear go through it because they under estimated it and never thought to see how deep it really is. This is also applicable to life because most of us make the mistake of downplaying important or dangerous things in life because their simplicity made us assume that they are not worth worrying about and end up regretting in the end.

So do not be quick to underestimate people and opportunities or potential dangers because you assumed they are nothing.

Congolese proverb

You cannot feast every day and become rich.

This Zulu proverb teaches about the importance of prudence, financial discipline and savings for the rainy days for everyone in life. The proverb teaches that no one gets rich by making money and throwing it away immediately on frivolities in life.

Budgeting and financial discipline are some crucial factors that must be adhered to by anyone who wishes to succeed and be financially free in life.

Pay attention to priorities, discard frivolities, panic spending and waste of resources no matter how free the money is flowing in. Tomorrow could be difficult.

South African proverb

When a man says yes, his Chi says yes too.

This rich Igbo proverb is rooted in the fact that one's mind and mentality is the foremost factors he must convince of his desire to become successful in life. And until he is on the same page with them, things will continue to fluctuate.

The proverb teaches that we most first believe in ourselves first before any other person believes in us to give us the opportunity to succeed.

You must have faith in yourself. You mustn't doubt yourself or feel inferior or unworthy. You are just as capable as any other person in this world.

The analogy of this proverb is derived from the fact that the Igbos believe that everyone has his own spirit or Chi which leads him or her. Here, this spirit or rather god stands for the mind and mentality.

Nigerian proverb

A big chair doesn't make one a king.

This Libyan proverb teaches us that respect and loyalty are earned and never bought or gotten out of intimidation and subjugation. Yes, you can be able to get respect with money or coercion, however, it will never last because you will lose it once your money stops flowing or you stop having an edge over the ones you are coercing.

Endeavor to be compassionate, sympathetic, and kind to people in all you do and in doing so; you will receive organic love and loyalty from people with integrity than throwing money or influence around and being surrounded by sycophants and parasitic people.

Libyan proverb

Yes, she is a beautiful lady but she must learn to work because she cannot eat beauty.

This proverb is mostly used by parents to caution their daughters about the dangers of assuming that all that matters in life are their pretty faces, round butts and pointed breasts. They use it to remind them to consider these factors secondary and work on their education, character, attitude, and management of wealth and home.

Zambian proverb

Yes, money cannot talk but it can definitely make a lie true.

Do not be deceived, money answereth all and it has the power to sway what people call justice and fairness.

This proverb is simply reminding us of the unfortunate fact which is that money can make people call a black pot a red one and will go to all lengths to say that it is a red pot even when everyone can clearly see that the pot is black. So, know where you seek the truth from.

The proverb is also used to remind both the young and old that it is vital that they try their best to have their own resources because it is what the world runs on. A lack of it totally makes one seem incapacitated.

Congolese proverb

Smooth seas never make skillful sailors.

Nothing great comes easy in life. This is a universal rule that have stood the test of time and many people that used it as their mantra have achieved great things in their fields and life just by acknowledging and affirming to this rule.

A farmer must soil his hands before he gets to harvest plenty produce during harvest time.

To be a doctor, you need to study and pass to be one. And it doesn't even finish their; you need to study more to perfect your craft, get more trainings, do more studies and researches, work hard and continue to get better because you become even better the more you grow. Believe me; I would rather have an aged doctor or nurse attend to me in a hospital than a younger person. This is also applicable to most jobs because one gets better and with experience comes better knowledge and trust from people that need your services.

Egyptian proverb

Dogs don't just prefer a bone to meat is just that no one gives them meat.

This great proverb is used to teach both the young and old that they should show compassion and empathy to the less privileged and poor around them because most of them weren't born or raised up in homes capable enough to support their ambitions so they fell to their current situations. Some of them worked harder, studied harder and gave their soul more than those that made it in life. It was just a case of luck. So, it is just human to be sympathetic to the unlucky ones because it could have been anyone.

Libyan proverb

The downfall of a nation begins in the people's homes.

Family is a great factor of the projection of the society at large. People with strong cultural background that recognizes the importance of strong family and marriage institution usually have a peaceful and stable society with less crime and low moral decadence.

Children that grew up in stable home of a father and a mom are usually responsible and patriotic than children raised by single parent or that were raised in a toxic home.

America, Europe should go back to the drawing board and know that the genesis of the unpatriotic nature of this generation and moral decadence is because of the strong institutionalized attack on the family and marriage institution.

Egyptian proverb

Your friend in the morning can become your worst enemy before the sun sets.

The human mind and heart is very strange and corny that it is unpredictable, especially when dealing with other humans. It's always about interests, which are sometimes selfish or selfless, mean, evil and very wicked. So, it is wise to be cautious and very protective of our mental, physical, financial and spiritual aspects of our lives while we make companions and stay with them. Do not open yourself so much that you become an open book to anyone. Sometimes, it is wise to be unpredictable and mysterious because every face that smiles in your face is not really friendly. Most are simply wolfs in sheep's clothing.

Moroccan proverb

The Almighty God created the land and gave it lakes and rivers so humans can live. The same God created the desert so human can find his soul.

This proverb right here is one of my favorite Kenyan proverbs because of its meaning and because it resonates with me that is a chronic introvert. Haha, don't blame me here.

The proverb simply uses the solitary nature of the deserts to teach us that it is good to sometimes isolate from the noise and rush of the world and deeply meditate and reflect so that we can have enough time to think properly and strategize our next moves and come out rejuvenated and ready to conquer.

So, it is ideal to have our alone time of sober reflection and thinking to understand how far we have come, our regrets, how we could have done it better and the future.

Kenyan proverb

The strength of the crocodile is in the water.

This great Congolese proverb teaches us to search within ourselves and recognize our strengths and weakness and strategize how to maximize it all for our good. Just like the crocodile that knows that its better chances of catching prey and surviving hugely depends on its relationship with the water. Hence, it lives there and hunts with the help of the water by catching its prey and drowning it first. So, the proverb is telling us to use all we have to survive in life.

Congolese proverb

The tongue is a two edged sword that cuts deeper than any blade.

Do not say anything while angry to your lover, colleague, family member, friend and those above us because once the words fly out from our mouth in such state, then it cannot be taken back.

Here, this Zulu proverb teaches us to watch our mouths lest we utter words that are capable of destroying life's, relationships, friendships, careers, families and businesses. So guard your mouth, speak only when you have something wise and useful to say.

South African proverb

Misfortune doesn't discriminate; it comes to everyone at some point in life.

This wise Togolese proverb teaches us to be strong and brave in the face of the adversities of life as it is just one of those things in life that we might not necessarily have control over.

Loss of a loved one is something we have no say over, disability from birth is something we have no power over, accidents are something we have no power over, sicknesses of any type are sometimes things we have no power over, misfortune and bad luck are also things we have no power over, heartbreak and natural disasters are also some of the things we have no power over. So, this proverb teaches us to not be crybabies when we are faced with these issues, rather, we should understand that it is just life happening to us and move forward.

Togolese proverb

Not everyone who chased the antelope caught it but he who caught it also chased it.

This great Liberian proverb teaches us the importance of making effort and trying while we then hope to succeed. We need to give our dreams a try, who knows the great things we can just end up achieving from by making little efforts?

Liberian proverb

A family tie is like a strong tree; during the storms, it can bend and not break.

We are stronger as a unit than as individuals.

This ancient proverb teaches us about the importance of family and union of likeminded individuals pursuing a particular goal.

As a student, try and make friends with highly passionate students that desires greatness as much as you desire it too because studying together and the uniqueness of different perspective will help push you.

Never walk alone in life because it is better to find your own tribe. Now, this tribe might not necessarily be your siblings or member of your extended family. What matters is that they want the same thing as you do. Their skin color, religion and background shouldn't be a problem as far as they share the same passion and have the potentials of helping you get better in life.

Moroccan proverb

There is no medicine strong enough to cure hatred and envy.

Hatred and envy have never helped any person achieve their aims in life. Instead, it fills you with bitterness and toxicity which makes you very unapproachable in life.

We, by all means must avoid the temptation of being envious of others because of their success, background, luck, position and achievements in life because it will never help us get to our own. We must try to be motivated and inspired by other's success and achievements to push harder and get our own.

Zimbabwe proverb

The wise never takes a step that is too long for his legs.

Strategy and proper planning will help you achieve your dreams faster and easier in life.

The lessons of this Rwandan proverb borders around the importance of proper thinking, research, understanding and planning in anything one chose to do in this life.

There is a due process to follow in most cases in the things we want and if we fail to adhere to this process, we will find ourselves to blame.

Rwandan proverb

You cannot convince a monkey that honey is sweeter than banana

This hilarious but wise proverb teaches us that in as much as it is good to give council to the fool; it is also wise to sometimes allow them to be properly taught a lesson by the consequences of their bad and foolish decisions.

Zambian proverb

He who wants to grow long teeth must first grow the lips to conceal it.

There are certain things that come with the level of success we aspire for or attain. Success and wealth or leadership often comes with its own challenges which are strong enough to knock someone that is not prepared off their feet.

We must prepare our mind and mentality to be able to handle critics, allegations, probe and scrutiny and even insults. Believe me; you will be fully tested by many people. They will push you to the wall and still push you even further. So, it is vital that you build the patience, the understanding and wisdom to outsmart them and their shenanigans.

Nigerian proverb

Before you go out with a widow, you must first inquire about what killed her late husband.

Things, histories and characters tend to repeat itself over the course of time. A fox will always be a fox regardless of how well it pretends to be a lamb.

This proverb is used to teach people to always pay attention to people's history. Especially in regards to criminality, abuse, bad character, addictions, and behavioral patterns. It is wise that we pay attention to these factors while dealing with people.

People don't just change overnight no matter how they claim they have. So, it is wise to conduct your own background study on people before you enter any kind of venture with them because doing so will help you avoid the calamities that will ensue from dealing with wolfs on sheep's clothing.

Zimbabwean proverb

To love someone who doesn't love you is like expecting the monkey to stop jumping from branch to branch.

Something's in life doesn't just change because of our wishes for them to change. We shouldn't make the mistake of thinking that we can make people change or that we can make them to adjust to accommodate us later in life when they had shown initial signs that they are simply not interested in us.

You can't force or love people into loving you in most cases. It is a risky venture that mostly leads to disappointment and heartbreaks. Look for the arms that are interested in having you in them and be with them than seeking out people that have no interest in you.

Congolese proverb.

No matter how in a hurry the buttock is, it will always be behind.

Something's in life never changes for no one. There are things that we must pass through, experience and see in life no matter how we try to avoid them. Such things are grief, heartbreak, and loss of money, the stress and pains of hard work, disappointments, betrayal and more.

It doesn't matter how we try to avoid them, one or the other will find its way to our life. So this proverb is used to teach people to expect these things and find a way to survive them so they wouldn't overwhelm us.

Ghana proverb

Love is love but love for self and family supersedes tall types of love.

There is no greater love than that which the Almighty God has for his children. The second most powerful love is that which a mother has for her child and the third is the love that exists among siblings.

Your family is your paradise on earth. It is where you go back to when life beats you black and blue. It is where you seek for support when you can't stand again.

Yes, some do have their problems but you are stronger with your family's love, support and prayers. There is none better than it. So make sure you keep it and if there is a fracas already, find a way to make amends and live as a union which you are.

Liberian proverb

It is he that goes to the toilet without wiping his buttocks that the housefly follows.

There are consequences to all we do in life. Most times these consequences come immediately while sometimes it comes later. However, it eventually finds its way to us.

If you decide to waste your productive years on frivolities and foolishness, the consequence of that decision is an old age of poverty and regrets.

If you see fire and still put your hands in it, it will surely burn you.

Try and make better decisions like eating healthy, exercising, going after your dreams and building a loving family today and wait for the benefits which entails good and healthy life, success and happiness that comes from good and strong family.

Ghana proverb

A housefly that perches on the scrotum is gently nudged and never struck.

There comes a time in the life of someone when the person needs to open his mind to a new horizon and look at issues from different perspectives. Your 9 could be another person's 6.

It also teaches that violence, aggression, being mean, being rude, being arrogant and cruel is not the only way to go through life. These are not the only way to get respect, loyalty and servitude from people. Humility, servitude, friendship, generosity, compassion and kindness can also earn you respect, loyalty and servitude from people.

Nigerian proverb

A wise fish should know that a worm floating on the river often has a sharp hook attached to it.

This particular proverb teaches us about the importance of being clever and street-wise while navigating life.

Everybody you deal with is looking for their daily bread and they may not mind getting it from your own pocket if need be.

Something's in life are just there to break us, we just need to see these things and find a way to live life while being clever. So, be vigilant while living your life. Do not trust easily. Think deeply while dealing with others. Do not take people's smiles in your face as a sign of absolute loyalty and trust. Pay good attention to people's history because it has a way of repeating itself. A fox will never become a lamb. Be careful.

Congolese proverb

If the sun says it's better than the moon, then let it shine at night.

The lesson in this proverb is all about the importance of people playing their roles without assuming they are more important than others.

The left hand and the right hand all have their roles to play regardless of the one the body choses to use more.

Life is like a game of football where everyone has their own designated roles. A striker has the role of scoring, attackers have the roles of creating opportunities for goals, midfielders has the role of controlling the tempo of the game to favor them, defenders has the role of protecting their box and keeper and stopping the opposition from scoring and the keeper has the role of not allowing the ball enter the goal post. Everyone who fails in his role brings defeat upon the team. Everyone is important and seeing it this way will help the team to conquer other teams. Apply this concept in life and you will attain greatness too.

Nigerian proverb

One can only advice the foolish, if he doesn't hear, let adversity teach him that which he refused to learn.

Everyone in life must not be successful or responsible. Some will still be used as example to warn the kids of the paths they shouldn't follow in life or turn out like such person.

We sometimes need to let the foolish, less ambitious, ignorant and unwise ones among us to be taught a lesson by poverty, starvation and other consequences of laziness, ignorance and uncalculated decisions.

Speak to them as much as you can. Advise them. Try to set people on the right path; if they refuse, let them be and let adversity cuddle them. Do not waste your precious time, energy and resources on someone that is ignorant and doesn't want to take advices and corrections.

Kenyan proverb

No matter how hot tempered you are; your hot temper cannot still boil an egg.

This is one of those hilarious but wise proverbs that African ancestors used to teach people that there is nowhere one is going with unnecessary anger issues.

The proverb teaches about the importance of one having control over self and not allowing anger and any other emotion put them in trouble.

It has always remained a fact that most actions humans carry out while angry are normally regretted once their heads cools off. So, find a way to have control over yourself. Avoid the things that trigger you before you make yourself a careless person who destroys and regrets later.

Ghana proverb

When the roots are deep in the ground; the tree has no reason to fear the wind.

This particular proverb talks about the importance of one having a very strong foundation in whatever they are doing in life. The proverb teaches that having such an edge in our career, education and life gives us an edge over others and prepares us to absorb the unforeseen and come back even stronger.

So try and get all the necessary trainings, studies, practical, researches and tools required in your field to be the best so you can be firm rooted in it and become good in it.

Malian proverb

When siblings fight to their death a stranger inherits their father's wealth.

Do not wash your dirty linens in public. What happens in Vegas should stay in Vegas too. Family and siblings do have their own problems sometimes. Some can be pure evil sometimes but they still share your blood and sucked the same breast that fed you. So, it is ideal that you do your best to stay together and in peace because believe me, they love you to death even if they try to hide it and show you tough love.

Settle your issues at home and let it not go to bed with you or be heard outside because you can never know who is interested in seeing your bond with your siblings broken.

Nigerian proverb

Seeing is better than being told.

Be certain about the nitty-gritty of an issue or situation about people or ventures before you share your opinions on it.

Our ancestors understood the dangers of one sided stories, hence they came up with this proverb admonishing people to hear, see and think about situations and ventures before they come to a conclusion about it.

So, do not be that person that will say things without proper understanding of the whole situation and later regret the things he had said when he later understands the whole situation. Listen properly, see clearly and reflect and ponder on things properly before sharing your opinions about them.

Cameroun proverb

Family must indeed look out for family.

No one should hear the cry of help of his sibling and look the other way. This is an unwritten rule that must never be broken. We all need to be there for those that we shared breast milk with.

Charity begins at home. So never abandon those you shared cries and laughter with while you were still a baby. They are your tribe, your community, and your own. Always be ready to offer succor if need be.

Make peace, drop ego and pride and call your sibling or better still visit them. Hug them and apologize for the issues and if they are the problem, go to them and tell them that you forgive them, hug them and tell them you miss them and you two shouldn't be fighting. Be at peace and unity with your family today. Find a way to make it work. Forgive your parents for their negligence or abuse so you can properly heal. Family is your greatest treasure.

Somali proverb

Even if the cock doesn't crow, the day must break.

Life doesn't revolve around you. In fact, you are inconsequential to the wheels of time and the ordinance of life. Humble yourself lest you be humbled in a bad way. Treat everyone with the respect and dignity they deserve as humans.

Where your wealth stops is actually where another person's own begins in life. The luxury cars you use to feel on top of the world are being driven by police officers in Dubai.

Life goes on with or without you regardless. So know that you are equal to other humans. In fact some are even better than you.

Moroccan proverb

You can only learn how to cut a tree down by cutting one down.

There is no better teacher in life than experience. You need to try and try again even if you fail, keep on trying at least you try each time with the knowledge of what to do and what not to do which you acquired from your previous mistakes.

You can't just wake up and become a pro in something without dedicating time to know the nitty-gritty of the thing you are doing. Failure actually is a great teacher because it betters us. So try cutting your first tree.

Congolese proverb

All we can do is to keep sacrificing and let the gods get all the blames.

This proverb is all about one doing what is meant for him to do while leaving the rest to his God.

If you want to be an athlete, you can't just lie on the bed and fantasize about being in the turf with the very best, no; rather you need to play your role which involves better dieting, intense workouts, constant practices and more. Once you have done all the vital things you need to do, then you now have the rights to pray to your God to help you achieve that which you have being working out for. Play your role first before looking up to God.

The analogy is derived from the fact that Africans are originally traditional people, so they are normally sacrificing livestock and farm produce to their gods to grant them favors, protection, wealth and good health. So, you are expected to make your sacrifices first and then when what you seek doesn't come you can then blame them. In other words, there is a price to be paid for everything and unless these prices are paid, what we seek for might never come.

Congolese proverb.

The Okro plant can never outgrow the planter.

The Okro is a popular vegetable that is very popular in West Africa and other parts of the world for its nutritious contents and its slimy and slippery texture. Once planted, within a while, the plant grows so tall, however, once the farmer wants to harvest, he simply bends the plant down, harvests and releases it again and cuts it off once it is done producing Okro. So, as the proverb implies; no matter how tall this plant grows, it still needs to be obedient to the man that planted, watered and weeded it. Same is also applicable to us about life. The proverb admonishes us about the importance of gratitude, humility, appreciation, and respect in life especially to our parents, sponsors, mentors, teachers, elderly, bosses and partners. It admonishes us not to be quick to forget those that made us whatever we are. It mostly admonishes us that it is our duty to take care of our parents when they become old and not to dump them to die in loneliness and heartbreak. It also teaches us not to disregard and disrespect those that made us to become successful in life.

Nigerian proverb

What else is expected of a stick of cigarette if not smoke?

Someone cannot give what he doesn't have. This brilliant Nigerian proverb teaches us about the importance of self-awareness, the importance of proper study of people that we deal with in all our daily endeavors. The proverb also teaches us the importance of carrying our dealings with people and on business with a full awareness of the history or past experiences. It is simply about us being smart and understanding that the back of a cooking pot will always be black and dirty so regardless of how people come at you with sweet tongues and pretense; it is vital you conduct yourself properly around them and also with their type of personality and character in mind so you will not be deceived or defrauded.

So, be very careful on how you treat and associate with people with records of criminal past and tendencies. Believe me; they are not going to change in your own time. Don't trust easily and always consult the past before you deal with people.

Nigerian proverb

Those that eat with spoons should be benevolent enough to remember those that eat with hands.

This proverb is all about appreciation, kindness, empathy, compassion, and generosity to those whose situations and conditions are dire and are going through life's rough terrains. The proverb admonishes everyone to not think that the world revolves around them alone and be kind enough to uplift the less privileged, render succor, put a smile on their face and to never look at the needy with disdain but to be grateful for what they have, help others and act with humility and empathy on those that are evidently below them.

Ghanaian proverb

Tallness and gray hairs are not proper yardsticks to measure maturity and wisdom.

Know who you listen to. This great proverb admonishes us to look beyond what the eyes can see when we go to people for counsel. The proverb teaches us that white hair doesn't necessarily mean wisdom, it reminds us that idiots and fools us grow old.

The analogy of this proverb is derived from the fact that old people are normally seen as wise people that are worthy of the ears of the youths in the African customs, however, this proverb is telling us that old age is not a yardstick to measure wisdom as fools also get old. In other words, we as a people needs to be very cautious of what will learn from people and try to avoid misfortunes by only listening to people who really know what they are talking about.

Nigerian proverb

My son, you must find the dark goat in the day time lest it gets dark.

This proverb is used to teach people about the importance of meticulous timing, strategy, understanding of situations and decisiveness in our dealings.

The proverb which is derived from the analogy of dark goats being almost invisible at night, hence, one must identify and separate them while it's still bright further teaches us that timing and preparedness are crucial parameters for success. To succeed in life or any field, you need to understand what you are getting into, you need to map out a realistic strategy to achieve it, you need to consistently follow this map, and finally, you need to work with time.

Nigerian proverb

Alila otherwise known as white ant is beautiful but the hen doesn't eat it.

As the Europeans will always say; "all that glitters is not gold." This great Nigerian proverb teaches us that everyone has a role to play in life. It also teaches that there is always a reason for everything. The great proverb also teaches that we shouldn't judge things and people simply by the smiles they wear or how nice they appear without a proper study and understanding. Hence, it is wise that everyone understands that things are not really as they seem.

For reference the analogy for this proverb is derived from an ant formerly called white ant or Alila by the Igbos of Nigeria. The white ant is beautiful compared to some other ants that the hens snack on but for some strange reasons, the hens do not eat the white ants even though they are beautiful.

Nigerian proverb.

When a cat steals a pot full of fishes it will start drinking tea.

Yes, it is a very funny one but it has great wisdom in it for counseling youths, new couples, and people that just came across a great fortune.

The proverb tries to teach us that it is common for new couples to overdo some things because of how sweet the new marriage is to them. Also, it is common to see a youth who suddenly made a fortune to start misbehaving because of the new sudden wealth, hence, the elders use this proverb to advise them that although they understand their new habits and misdeeds, however, many have that part and failed so they should remain focused, calm and walk and carry out their activities with caution.

The analogy is derived from the fact that cats and other pets like dogs or domestic animals are usually left to fend for themselves in the ancient African settings and cats always tend to start misbehaving or eating weirdly once they over feed thinking that it will be so forever.

Gambian proverb.

Tell a child to wash his body and he will wash only his stomach.

One cannot offer what he doesn't have. This great African proverb advices us to not expect too much from people especially when we don't know them so well. Life is a tricky journey and the heart of men are so corny and tricky so much that we cannot possibly tell what they are thinking or what their true intentions are. So this proverb teaches us that we should always look out for patterns of behaviors from people. Always look out for people's past history. Always pay attention to people and their manipulative stages. A fox will always be a fox.

Zambian proverb.

If a snake fails to show its venom, little kids will use it and tie firewood.

One must not over simplify himself to the stage that people take advantage of their simplicity and manipulate them. You must not present yourself to be so soft to people.

This proverb teaches us that there is a difference between humility and softness and naivety. We, as a people must learn to differentiate between these and be cautious of who we show our soft side to or who we show our vulnerabilities.

The analogy for this proverb is derived from the fact that ancient African people are naturally gatherers and their major source of energy is firewood. So, to get this firewood, kids and women enter the bush and gather these dry sticks they use for firewood and find a rope to tie before they take it home. So if the snake doesn't show what it is the kids will use it to tie their firewood, so to avoid that, the snake needs to bite them. Such is also applicable to man in his dealings with other men.

Ghanaian proverb

There are many leafs in the bush but people go into the bush to look for Ukazi leaf.

The Ukazi leaf is a popular vegetable used by the Igbos to make most of their soups and other delicious delicacies. So based on this analogy, the proverb is saying that although that there are other leaves in the bush, still people only go to pick only the Ukazi which is the valuable one amongst them. Hence, this proverb is teaching us that we should always endeavor to make ourselves valuable and possibly the best in whatever we are doing in life so we can always standout from the crowd, hence, positioning ourselves for better promotions, better jobs and pays. The proverb also teaches us about the importance of prioritizing and going after that which we so desire regardless of the thorns and challenges on the way.

Nigerian proverb.

Someone suffering from severe diarrhea doesn't have the luxury of selecting toilets.

This proverb is used to remind us that there is no greater teacher in life than empty pocket and starving tummy. This is derived from the fact that one that is starving and broke is often overwhelmed by the reality at hand and has time to reflect on his mistakes and places he can improve not to starve and be broke again. So, failure is not always as bad as it looks because it has a way of aggressively waking people from their slumber.

Nigerian proverb

The woman that is seeking for a child never goes to bed wearing a pant.

Opportunity likes the company of the prepared one. You can't just stay at a place and be expecting miracles to happen for you without putting the required effort to achieve your aims. Life doesn't work like that and things will not change for you. You need to put in the required hard work, consistency and preparedness to take the bull by the horn when the bull comes around.

Skill up, get the necessary certificates and trainings you need to move up the ladder in your work and be ready for when the opportunity comes because it will surely come.

Nigerian proverb.

A snake must birth something that is long and venomous.

This great proverb is used to teach people about the importance of paying attention to the background and history of the people you deal with in life. This is also applicable to people in businesses. Endeavor to do your own consultation and due diligence on things before you commit your emotions, resources or time to it.

A person that has a history of criminality and dubious acts stands a great chance to repeat such characters in the feature. So, it is either you study them and identify the red flag and let them go or you will be their victim.

This is also applicable when we are choosing or romantic or business partners. Know the history of your partner, identify their red flags early and decide within you to continue or leave before you meet your doom. A cheater will always cheat once the chance comes. A liar and chronic manipulator will always show up once the opportunity presents itself.

This reminds me of people that drags people out of their marriage to marry them thinking that similar fate will not befall them. Just know that history always has a way of repeating itself. So make the right choices today and avoid your doom and regrets tomorrow.

Egyptian proverb

You should not suffocate me because I told you to lean on me.

The lesson in this proverb is about the importance of knowing when to apply caution and not over beg for any kind of support, not to be so reliant on someone for support that we turn a blind eye to their own pains.

There should be a limit to what we expect from people. Do not lose the little dignity you have in the eyes of the people you run to for help by abusing their generosity. Be smart to use the second chances people give you for good than still messing everything up and still running back to the same people for help. You need to understand that people also have their own problems. So, respect yourself and do not abuse people's kindness to you.

Rwandan proverb

It is trusting blindly that made the fish to boil to death in a pot of water.

Do not trust people easily. Learn to be stingy with giving out your trusts and how strong you believe in the promises or the words of people.

People will go any length to satisfy their interests and this length includes fraud, criminality and other things. So, you need to trust less and follow your instincts and facts.

Rwandan proverb

I heard what you said doesn't mean I agree with you.

This particular proverb teaches the importance of proper understanding of people's intentions, words, actions, behaviors and motives before drawing conclusion on them.

Do not be too hasty to assume what someone means. Try and pay attention to them firstly, let them finish, ask questions if you are confused and be certain that what you think is actually what they mean before you present a different thing or quote them out of context.

Algerian proverb

Water and liquor has the same color but they are not the same thing.

Be patient and smart enough to think through things and be certain of the situation or the type of people you are dealing with before you commit yourself. Do not be easily deceived by the pretentious lives of some people you may meet while conducting your dealings.

Everyone is only interested in what is in for them. So know this and know peace and apply wisdom accordingly lest you become a fool for them.

Disregard how innocent or honest they might look initially or even their eloquence. Leave all that and follow your heart and instincts and what you found out about them in your own little studies.

Beware of wolfs in sheep's clothing.

Zambian proverb

You don't learn to use your left hand in your old age.

There is always time for everything under the sun. Times lost on frivolities or insignificant escapades are never recovered.

If you waste your productive years on nonsense, you will never recover the time lost and before you know it you become old and die of regrets and poverty.

If you waste the time you need to use to study and learn a craft to party, time will come when you can't go back to learn and everything will become late and regrets will be your soul mate.

So why not make haste why the sun shines now and follow the due process to your success and don't try to jump steps lest you break your legs.

Burundi proverb

The child that loves party rice shouldn't be afraid of dance.

There are prices to pay for whatever we want out of life. So this proverb is teaching us not to shy away from these prices if indeed we really want to achieve our aims.

You can't just fantasize about something and it will come to you. Life doesn't work like that. You are expected to study about the requirements for that goal and carry out those requirements before you get to the goal. It is just as simple as that and there often no shortcuts around it. In most cases, these factors or rather requirements are usually, studies, researches, consistency, dedication, passion, focus, hard work and purpose.

Nigerian proverb

He who holds another person in the ground still holds himself too.

No one progresses by devoting their entire time on schemes and plots for the downfall of another person either in work, academics or any other field of life.

We may not know it but we somehow get consumed by the evil we plan for others. Yes, this is a fact because one that fills himself with negativity, envy, jealousy, wickedness and evil somehow shows these qualities in whatever they do. So, it is ideal that we forget about dragging people down and use that energy and time and focus on making ourselves better because we will never progress if all we think about is how to destroy others.

Nigerian proverb

How you do anything is how you do everything.

The little things we do when no eyes are on us matters a lot. How you conduct yourself doing little things like dressing your bed after sleep, doing your laundry, keeping your environment and home neat, the kindness you show to the needy when camera is not around, those you offer help to even when you know they can't repair and many more little things has a huge influence on your personality and actions.

So, discipline yourself to not deceive yourself by doing eye-service but being the same person in private or public.

Ethiopian proverb

A man without purpose is nothing but a dry leaf in the desert.

This proverb teaches about the importance of every person finding a purpose in life to help them remain focused in pushing for a better life for them and the people around them.

One without purpose is simple a waste of oxygen and space. You offer no relevance, you become a liability to those around you because you have no future, because nothing wakes you up in the morning, there is no ambition, there is no drive, there is nothing to work on. You simply exist to eat and defecate. And that is one mediocre life not worth living.

Ethiopian proverb

We fight a battle against death every day. Sadly, it will win one day.

Death is practically inevitable. It is a call that every person must answer sometime regardless of the person's class, religion, disability, race, and deeds. We all must die one day. And the scary part is that we do not know the second, minute, hour or day it will be. However, it must come. So, how about we endeavor to live a life worth celebrating when we are no more. How about we live a legacy that will be used to remember us when we are gone. It is actually no brainer.

So be compassionate, kind, sympathetic, be humble, be generous, build great bonds with others, create a strong and loving family that will remember and cherish you for eternity.

Desist from arrogance, pride, wickedness, intimidation, and greed,

Moroccan proverb

The harder one works, the luckier he becomes.

Someone that has spent some good time developing himself and learning important skill is always called a lucky one when the opportunities that he has been preparing for starts coming.

This proverb is simply trying to teach us to skill-up, learn the necessary things we need, practice and practice until we become good at something so we can be ready to be taking the opportunities as they come.

Ethiopian proverb

Fast wealth comes with slow and bigger tragedies.

There are always dire consequences in cutting corners to attain greatness in life. Life is so mean when it decides to punish you for trying to put a stone to the natural wheel of things. And the tricky part about it all is that some of these consequences take time to manifest. So, it is tricky because the person that cut corners could be all happy and merry for the main time and even when the consequences arrive, he may think it is another thing not knowing that mother nature have come to ask questions.

You cannot cut corners to be an athlete in life. Even if you do, the consequences will be embarrassment on the turf and a mediocre career.

You cannot corners to graduate from your studies. Even if you cut, the consequences will be a mediocre career. The list is actually endless.

So, this proverb teaches us to avoid the temptations of following the shortcuts and put in the required hard work to attain the success we desire.

South African proverb

If your own house doesn't put you up for sale, no outsider will buy you.

Your betrayal will always come from within. It is always one of the persons that know you better that will sale you out to the highest bidder.

So, in order not to be an open book to your adversaries, you should protect yourself by not being too predictable. Do not reveal more than necessary to people around you. Fully know the background of people around you. Do not trust easily too.

Ghana proverb

He who desires to have no challenges in life must seek to be born on another planet.

It is not a secret that life is ruthless and respecter of none.

Life has no special treatment for you. It is expected that everyone fully understands this very early in life and know that they have to fight, struggle, work hard and have sleepless nights just to get what they desire out of life.

Life has no regards for lazy, entitled, delusional people that are not ready to carve out their destiny by their hands. So, if you want a place without stress, maybe you should have asked your parents to give birth to you on planet Pluto. Maybe the extraterrestrials there will accommodate your lazy ass or maybe not.

Ugandan proverb

The glow of the firewood soon turns into ashes.

Beauty and handsomeness never last in life. There will come a time when the beauty of youthfulness will go and the body will become old and fragile. At this time, no one will care about how pretty you were in your youth. What will now matter will be how good you have lived? What you have achieved. The family you have built and the way you are going to live out the rest of your life on earth.

So, this proverb here is used to teach people to place secondary priority on these qualities that expire but build on their life, career, family and retirement before it becomes very late.

Algerian proverb

Water will always be wet.

Something's never change. Some people never change also.

This proverb is trying to teach us to always pay attention to the history and patterns of people's behavior because in one way or the other, it will still repeat in the future.

Do not pay attention to the "I have changed BS." A fox will always be a fox no matter how long it disguises or pretends to be a sheep.

Never be caught unguarded. Stay vigilant and smart.

South African proverb

A master can only point in one way; its only experience that will make you great.

No one is going to help you marry a wife and also help you impregnate her. Your parents will not be here for eternity to help you. You need to now take control of your life and take the guidance and instructions and education you have had and make a name for yourself. You mustn't depend on people that much. People can only carry you so far. You need to carve out your own destiny on your own terms.

Kenyan proverb.

It is the rat inside that informed the rat outside that there is a fish in the pot.

This particular proverb teaches us that betrayals in life often come from the people within. There is no way a stranger will plot and succeed on taking you down without the help of those within. So, it is vital that we are very meticulous and careful about the kind of people we keep around us or that know our weaknesses.

Life is a game where only the strong and cautious ones succeed. Don't assume that there are not those that are plotting and scheming for your downfall. It is wise that we have this idea and then know who to surround ourselves with or who we reveal certain things to lest we get caught unguarded.

Nigerian proverb

Winds do not blow as the ship wishes.

Life doesn't care about your struggles, limitations, disabilities, sicknesses, race, religion, background or your feelings. It moves as it wants and has no time to wait for anyone to keep up.

Your life and destiny are in your hands to make of it whatever you want only if you are ready to put in the required efforts, dedication, hard work, consistency and focus.

It is only that can define your future. No spiritual being is coming for your safety or succor. You are your own helper, comforter, motivator, inspirer and best fan.

Stop expecting help of any kind from people. Never be entitled about people's success no matter who the person is to you or what you have done for the person before.

Egyptian proverb

He who ventures into uncharted waters will meet doom or discover chests of treasure.

Yes, it is good to take risks in life. However it is very bad to take uncalculated risks in life.

You can't just enter the desert without prior knowledge of how to survive under such harsh conditions.

You cannot venture into any business without a proper study and consultation about the nature of it. Doing so without a sound knowledge of what you are doing only means loss and disappointments.

So, do your due diligence about people and business, career, lifestyle, decisions, studies, people, friendships, partners and more. Meticulously survey, consult and understand whatever you plan to go after before you meet your doom by making uncalculated moves.

Egyptian proverb

A boat with two captains will surely sink.

This particular proverb is all about setting priorities in what is more important and who is more important in our lives and giving them time according to relevance to us.

Your life is the boat and the things you spend your time on are the captains. There should be a balance and proper time and energy allocation for these things.

There should be a proper balance of time between your career and family. One who is more interested in career will find himself losing his or her family. So this proverb is teaching us to find a way to balance these things lest we sink the ship.

Egyptian proverb

On the top of a beautiful woman, a man will promise more than what God created.

This proverb teaches us to expect less from people and their promises. The proverb tries to make us understand that people will use any means possible to get what they want from you. They don't mind promising you heaven and earth just to get what they want. So it is vital that we think properly while dealing with people and be smart enough to know when they are simply saying things or doing things to get what they selfishly want from us.

Zimbabwean proverb.

None is blinder than he who doesn't want to see.

Someone who doesn't want to do something for you will find any reason available to not do that. So, it is wise we expect little from people and have contingency plans in case we meet desperate and dishonest people that are ready to lie under oath just for their selfish interests.

Moroccan proverb

A contented mind is a hidden treasure and trouble finds it not.

A contented man is one that has conquered greed. We as a people must learn to be happy, contented with only that which our incomes can afford. We shouldn't lose our integrity, moral compass and soul to greed and the ever unquenchable hunger for more even to the extent of being envious of other people's belongings.

Be appreciative of the little you have. Remove your eyes from people's properties, beautiful partners and lifestyle. Go and work and earn enough to earn any lifestyle you desire.

Egyptian proverb

One must not wash his dirty linen in public.

There is no household without their qualms and disagreements between siblings. It is natural to have sibling rivalry especially between the old and young or opposite genders. However, what matters is that it ends as simple as a tough love type of rivalry which results to laughers and jokes.

Siblings, romantic partners, business partners or friends should endeavor to settle their issues and disagreements within themselves without taking their issues to the public.

Egyptian proverb

**He who has not cultivated his fields must
not hope for a better harvest.**

You reap where you sow. Nothing in life comes to the
lazy and unprepared people.

If you waste your productive years wasting your time
on unproductive ventures, it is almost certain that
such a person will live out the remaining days of his
life under poverty and with heavy regrets. You don't sit
with arms folded from morning till night and have the
audacity to complain when you have no food to eat.

Get up from your sit today and get busy with your life
and find a way to survive and progress so you can make
a living for yourself.

Niger proverb.

Too many cooks spoil the porridge.

Too much salt in a dish doesn't make it sweet rather it defeats the purpose which is to make it eatable.

This proverb teaches us that we must be very cautious not to overdo things in life lest we defeat the purpose of doing the thing at the first place.

Be kind but don't be more than necessary lest people take advantage of you. Focus on your career but don't overdo it lest you lose focus of your relationship with your children, partners, siblings and friends or even lose yourself.

Focus on your studies but still create time for fun and fostering relationship with the ones that care about you. Be friendly but don't overdo it so people will not see you as desperate, weird or take advantage of you.

Senegalese proverb

Never leave till tomorrow that which you can do today.

Complacency and procrastination are the greatest hindrances of personal growth and success in life.

Resist laziness, complacency and procrastination like a plague and you will see yourself perform better and improve in all ramifications of your career or studies.

Ethiopian proverb

None knows the weight of another man's burden.

You are never the most unfortunate person in life. No matter what you are going through, you must find the heart to still be grateful for the things you have and the breath of life. People have it way harder than you.

Do not be a cry baby about the challenges you are facing. Just find a way to survive because thousands of people if not millions has it way harder than you. Be grateful and find a way to survive.

Ghana proverb

If life shows you pepper, make pepper soup out of it.

This proverb teaches us to take advantage of whatever life brings our way and find a way to survive regardless of how tough or challenging it is.

Do not be a cry baby about your tough experiences in life. You are actually having it easier than others. Find a way to keep your head up and always know that life doesn't care about your tears or feelings. You must find a way to survive.

Nigerian proverb.

I used to be rich before is what we all pray against.

This proverb is used to teach people that wealth and riches never last in the hands of one that has no desire to multiply it and enlarge it. The proverb teaches that money is quick to leave the hands of a fool if he doesn't try to protect and multiply it. Hence, it is a very important prayer here because life becomes literally unbearable when someone who used to be rich becomes poor because of their carelessness. So, we should know that wealth finishes if it is not properly managed.

Nigeria proverb

A good name is better than all the gold and silver in the world.

This life is never all about money and authority. Sometimes a good name paves a way for one and his generations unborn.

As you journey through life, endeavor to live a good life with integrity, sincerity, servitude, compassion, humility, respect and kindness. You might think that nobody is noticing you but you will be surprised how people are secretly revering you and how your good name is paving ways for you.

Egyptian proverb.

The poor man has no reservation in the village meeting.

It is no secret that life is so cruel for the less privileged, especially those without money. Believe me; no one will genuinely respect you and your admonitions. That is just life. So you must endeavor to find a legal way to make it in life so you can at least keep your dignity as a human in the gathering of people. However, we all can't have money but we should endeavor to be useful at least in one important thing in life. You can't be poor and useless.

Ghana proverb

Don't wait for the table to turn for you; simply change sits if it doesn't.

This proverb teaches us about the importance of taking our own destinies in our own hands and not limiting our potentials because of limitations like lack of education, racism, religion, family background, gender, disability or region. Be bold and go after that which you so desire no matter the hurdles on the way.

Nigerian proverb.

The gentle strides of the tiger never indicate cowardice.

This proverb teaches us the importance of not understating anyone or task in life. It also teaches us to be humble while dealing with people we perceive to be below us lest they embarrass us.

Give respect to everyone and treat everyone with the respect and dignity they deserve as human.

Nigerian proverb

One cannot run and scratch his stomach the same time.

This Nigerian proverb teaches us the importance carrying out our activities in life based on priorities and values of each task. We cannot waste our time being Jack of all trades. We must as a matter of fact focus our energy and resources on one field and trying to be the go to name for that. You cannot serve two masters at a time. It is easy to focus on one and become highly good at that than wasting your energy, time and resources on many things and ending up becoming an average person on everything.

Nigerian proverb.

He who fetches ants infested firewood inside his house is inviting the lizard in too.

This proverb teaches us that there are consequences for the things we do in this life. Cause and effects is a thing in life. Hence, we must be cautious to do the things that will not be detrimental to us in any manner later in life.

If you waste your youth partying and chasing girls up and down without investing in bettering your life and making a name for yourself, you will end up being broke and miserable when old age comes.

The analogy for this proverb is gotten from the fact that most tree branches where we get are firewood from often gets infested with ants once they start drying. So the proverb is telling us that if we get this firewood and keep them in the room instead of outside; we should expect ants on our bed.

Nigerian proverb

How can we identify the lizard with stomach ache since all of them lies with their bellies?

This great proverb teaches us the importance of being bold and outspoken in life. The proverb teaches us to avoid being timid and shy in life because being like that will keep us away from many opportunities in life.

Think about it; how will your helper know what you need if you are not bold enough to talk or at least indicate that you need help. Being shy should end while we are kids, we should all put it away as we grow because it will not give us any good thing in life but regrets and sadness. Imagine walking pass your crush every day because you couldn't say a word and she later relocates or start dating your sibling. It will be painful right? Just raise your head and approach the person, the worst she can say is 'no' and if she says 'eww' just take it like a man and move on. Well, jokes apart now, we need to say our mind sometimes. Speak your mind and move.

Ghana proverb

The fish that doesn't eat other fishes will never grow fat.

This great Malawian proverb teaches us the importance ruthlessness, strict discipline, and focus in achieving our objective goals in life. The proverb teaches us that the world and its goodies are never for the faint hearted or timid. As the Gen Z's will always say, "the street is military, only the strong will survive."

Sometimes, we need to show our tough side to avoid people perceiving us as naïve and taking advantage of us. Believe me, humans likes to ride on the meek and soft hearted. So, try to differentiate between naivety and humbleness. Be cat when you have to and also roar like the loudest lion when the needs arises lest people manipulate you.

Ethiopian proverb.

It is the head that disturbs the nest of the wasps that the wasps stings.

It is called cause and effects. There are consequences for a every decision, actions and lifestyle one choses to live.

This great Congolese proverb teaches us that we must be ready to accept the consequences of all our actions, decisions and choices in life. It teaches that there is no supernatural power that is stopping us from greatness but only our choices in life.

So make better and sound choices with your companions, lifestyle, partner, job, residency, mentors and idols, education and you will reap the sweet fruits.

Congolese proverb.

It is the deity that people worships that kills them.

You are what you eat. One can only give out what he has.

This great Senegalese proverb teaches us that we are mostly a reflection of what we spend our time and life doing. Someone who eats carelessly will grow fat and develop sickness related to careless eating and fatness. One who drinks too much will develop vital organs issues. One who womanizes will have unwanted pregnancies, and STDs. One who takes a lot of sugar will have diabetes. Also, one who exercises a lot will reap the benefits of a healthy body and sound mind. One who studies a lot will be a pro in his field. An athlete that is the hardest worker in the room will have the major accolades. One who eats properly will have a nice body and health. In other words, you will reap from whatever you spend your time on in your youthful days. So, you are the maker or breaker of your greatness in life because what you do today determines how you will end up tomorrow.

Senegalese proverb.

The chicken says that the reason it looks up while drinking water is because what kills its chickens always comes from the sky.

This Cameroun proverb is used to admonish both the old and the young to always pay attention to history, experiences and patterns of behaviors of people, siblings, colleagues, partners, workers, business and most of the things we do in life. The essence of this strict warning lies in the fact that a fox will always be a fox, a snake will always do what it has to do to eat. Same thing applies to us human because one who has shown greed, criminal, fraudulent, manipulative tendencies in the past will always exhibit such attitudes in the future, so follow such people with all cautiousness and never relent in being watchful of when they will strike again.

A woman or man who cheated their self to be your partner has the tendency to cheat to a new partner again. So as the chicken, always look while drinking water because what kills its chicks always comes from the sky, you too should also be vigilant.

Cameroun proverb

**The king that kills his greatest warrior
because he mistakenly poured the king's
keg of palm wine away; what will he now
do when his kingdom is invaded
tomorrow?**

This proverb teaches us the importance of careful thoughts before actions. It teaches us the importance of strategy and meticulous planning of our activities, actions, utterances, partnerships and every other thing that will in one way or the other affects our lives.

It also teaches us not to make hasty decisions in anger or without proper evaluations of the consequences.

Cameroun proverb.

The he-goat that died in the barn full of yams was not killed by hunger.

It is important that we pay attention to details and fully understand the circumstances surrounding every incident, situations before we make our judgments.

This proverb also teaches us that laziness will be the undoing of many people but more importantly, it teaches us to always approach situations or gossips about people meticulously so we can fully understand the full situation before making our decisions.

The analogy of the proverb is derived from the fact that ancient Africans are usually farmers and gatherers. And they are known to have goats at home and they also have their own barns full of yams. Now, the yam is the goat's favorite snack whether cooked or not. So, for any goat to die inside a barn of full of yam, hunger is definitely not what killed it.

Niger proverb.

My son, you are expected to salute the deaf; if the heavens don't hear, the earth will.

This South African proverb teaches the importance of respect, empathy and kindness towards others. The proverb also teaches us to always do the right thing with or without the flashlights of the camera. Yes, you can actually help the needy in whichever capacity you can without making praise songs for yourself and posting it for the whole world to see and validate your charitable actions.

South African proverb.

A palm nut that wants to be a palm oil must first pass through the fire.

There is a process to achieve any great feat in life.

This great Nigerian proverb admonishes us about the importance of due process and perseverance in our daily activities in pursuit of our different individual aspirations. This proverb also teaches us that there are necessarily no shortcuts to greatness in life. So to achieve your dreams, you must study, understand what it takes, and consistently dedicate your time, energy, resources towards achieving it. If you want to be an athlete, you must first change your diet, your lifestyle, out work every other person in the room and consistently practice to get better and stay fit and be ready to hit the turf and win your accolades. You can't just wish things to fruition. No, something has to give. A price must be paid.

Nigerian proverb.

The man that implores aggression in his dealings with others is afraid of reasoning.

One who has nothing to say makes the loudest noise in a room full of men. This Ethiopian proverb teaches to be careful not to waste our precious time indulging fools in their foolish arguments lest they bring us den to their stupidity.

According to the proverb, it is always those that have nothing meaningful or wise to offer in a discussion that goes on ranting on top of their voices and might even implore physical violence to make their points. So the proverb implores us to avoid such characters. It also implores us to shut our mouth and listen if we have nothing meaningful to contribute to a discussion.

Ethiopian proverb.

If the roots of the Iroko tree are not watered, the Iroko tree will not be mighty.

There is a price to pay to achieve greatness and wealth in life. It is a give and take pattern.

The Igbo people of the Eastern region of Nigeria are people known for their high business acumen and the potential to develop any place they travel to. These people in their experiences with life and wealth and what it takes to achieve greatness coined this proverb to admonish both their young and old that nothing in life is for free, hence, you must as a matter of fact be ready to put in the required effort to achieve your objections.

The analogy for this proverb is derived from the fact that the Iroko tree which is a sacred and mighty tree in most African region is known for its tallness and grace in the midst of other trees. The tree is so sacred that many make their gods and the objects they use in their worship from it but all its usefulness will not be possible if the tree wasn't properly watered while growing up.

Nigerian proverb.

**The hunter who walks slowly will not step
on thorns and his games will be plenty.**

This great Somalia proverb teaches us the importance
of patience in life. Patience is a very important element
in achieving great success in life. Haste exposes one to
uncalculated moves and unending failures in life.

We, as a people must be cautious enough to always be
patient in life so we can have time to plan our moves
so we will not meet failure in our parts in life.

Somalia proverb.

Don't meddle with a family or lover's issue lest they use you and settle their problem.

This Nigerian proverb is used to teach people to always know their boundaries in people's lives lest they get too comfortable and overstep their boundaries.

Again, the proverb teaches us not to involve ourselves in what we don't have sufficient information about, especially cases between friends and lovers lest they settle and see you as the weapon of separation that have been fashioned against them.

Nigerian proverb

www.ingramcontent.com/pod-product-compliance
Lightning Source LLC
Chambersburg PA
CBHW061031250726
48653CB00001B/48